THE UPSTART GUIDE TO
Owning and Managing a Bed & Breakfast

Lisa Angowski Rogak

UPSTART PUBLISHING COMPANY, INC.

Published by Upstart Publishing Company, Inc.
a division of Dearborn Publishing Group, Inc.
155 North Wacker Drive
Chicago, Illinois 60606-1719
(800)235-8866 or (312)836-4400

Neither the author nor the publisher of this book is engaged in rendering, by the sale of this book, legal, accounting, or other professional services. The reader is encouraged to employ the services of a competent professional in such matters.

Library of Congress Cataloging-in-Publication Data
Rogak, Lisa Angowski.
    The upstart guide to owning and managing a bed and breakfast / Lisa Angowski Rogak.
        p.   cm.
    Included index.
    ISBN 0-936894-65-2
    1. Bed and breakfast accommodations—Management. 2. Hotel management. I. Title.
TX911.3.M27R627 1995
647.947303'068—dc20   94-29629
                                                    CIP

Cover design by Paul Perlow Design, New York, NY.
Back cover photo by David Parker.

Printed in the United States of America
10 9 8 7 6 5 4 3

For a complete catalog of Upstart's small business publications, call (800) 235-8866.

For the Stomper Dolls

CONTENTS

PREFACE

I know what you must be thinking as you pick up this book. You've probably stayed in a B&B or two—or a hundred—over the years. Your hosts were friendly and content with what they were doing. It probably seems that running a B&B would make for a much easier lifestyle than the kind you're living now, and happier as well. I mean, what would be better than earning your living by spending time with interesting people from all over the world who pay you to stay in your home; creating hearty breakfasts and watching everyone clean their plate before sharing the best of your town and area with your guests? All you'd have to do, it seems, is crack a few eggs in the morning and make a few beds in the afternoon. The rest of your time you'll spend socializing. What could be easier?

If you believe this fantasy, well, the B&B owners profiled in this book are here to tell you that it ain't necessarily so. Opening a B&B is a pleasant and hospitable business, but there's a lot of hard work hidden behind it. In this book, I'll show you a glimmer of what it's all about, but I'll warn you in advance that it won't be until you plunge right into the preparations of taking in your first guest that you'll say, "Oh, *this* is what they were talking about!"

If you love people and tend to be a homebody, a B&B will be a great business for you to own and operate. But you also need some business acumen to successfully run a B&B, and it will probably consume more time and energy than you thought.

That's where this book comes in. I will show you how to set up and organize your business so that you'll be able to spend more time on the fun part of running your B&B—visiting with guests, decorating, and cooking—all interests that bring most people into the business in the first place.

As a travel writer specializing in B&Bs and small inns, I've met hundreds of B&B hosts whose hospitality and enthusiasm constantly shine through despite the long hours and hard work. How do they do it? Each draws on a different source to get through the tough times, but they do all share one thing in common: they love people and enjoy making them happy. True, your intentions in wanting to start your own B&B may be selfish—perhaps you crave a change in your lifestyle, a move to the country—but if you aren't ready to be in a position of service to your guests, then you'd better think twice. Operating a B&B is hard work, and many times it's the graciousness and appreciation of your guests that will save you when it seems you're running on fumes.

Or so I've heard. My partner and I talk of starting our own B&B somewhere down the road. I feel I've had a great education so far—visiting scores of B&Bs as well as writing this book—but I know that I won't truly get a sense of what it's all about until our first guest walks through the door.

And then, like you, I'll hit the ground running.

OPPORTUNITIES

A bed-and-breakfast is one of the few businesses where you don't have to be particularly mindful of the customers' needs when you're first starting out. You can decorate your house in the style you want and serve the kind of breakfast that you prefer.

This may sound counterintuitive, but let me explain. If you've visited any number of B&Bs, you've seen that each has its own personality. Yes, perhaps the oversized thirsty towels were selected with guests in mind as well as the gazebo out back, but the feel of the place reflects the likes and desires of the owners, and not what the owners think the guests would like.

In an age where the "customer is always right" and businesses bend over backwards to serve them, this attitude of Owner First may seem like an anomaly of sorts. But consider this: in a time when people feel overwhelmed by the sheer number of choices, as well as dismayed by the cookie-cutter themes endemic to most chain hotels, guests who choose to stay in B&Bs actually welcome the chance to be taken by the hand and told, "This is the way it is." And of course, once they find a B&B that suits them, they'll return.

Now, let me add that one way in which the B&B guest will always be right is in regards to service. One big thing that

B&B guests like best is to have a good reading lamp with a strong wattage light bulb right by the bed. Easy, right? But sometimes B&B owners get so caught up with making their house and guest rooms conform to their own personal vision, in the way of decorations and furnishings, that they overlook the practical things, like having a good reading lamp on the nightstand.

One of the best suggestions to a B&B owner is that they occasionally spend the night in one of their guest rooms. This, more than anything else, will—pardon me—throw some light on what it's really like to be a guest at your B&B.

Green Hill Farm

You'll find Nuna and Ted Cass at the 35-acre Green Hill Farm in Ashville, Maine, a three-room B&B and a farm, with angora rabbits, five sheep, a vegetable garden, and an apple orchard. The farm's size is plenty for Nuna, but not for Ted, who grew up in Iowa on what he says, "constitutes a farm."

Nuna and Ted moved to Maine in 1985. Nuna kept six sheep back in Iowa while Ted taught high school Spanish. When they moved to Ashville they specifically sought a house with room for a seasonal B&B, themselves, and assorted animals; though as Nuna jokes, "We started the B&B because we had too many blankets." They started the B&B in 1987 and found the transition to be effortless since they were accustomed to having a variety of people living in their house; back in Iowa they took in a number of foreign and exchange students.

Green Hill has two bedrooms with a shared bath available for guests. One room has a three-quarter bed, a rocker, and a cottage pine dresser; the other room has two twin beds. The bedrooms are located just off a second-floor landing that is extra wide. The house used to be a center chimney cape, and what's now a staircase with a shiny banister used to accommodate a chimney.

Nuna serves a traditional country breakfast and asks guests the night before if they want French toast, omelets, muffins, or just coffee and juice. She tells of guests who have worked their way up the Maine Coast visiting other B&Bs, and by the time they reach Green Hill in northern Maine, all they want is toast and coffee. Nuna is happy to oblige them.

The Casses started the B&B without knowing they were carrying on a longtime tradition on the farm. The original Route 1 ran right past the house, and Green Hill had previously served as a popular tourist home in the 1920s and 1930s. In fact, Nuna found an old sign in the attic that advertised rooms and meals in the farmhouse. Built in 1820, the house had remained in the same family until the Casses bought it.

Nuna likes to do the chores before guests get up, though she encourages guests to help put hay in the feeder and carry water out to the sheep. Because sheep can be very skittish around strangers, she suggests that guests take a few slices of bread to make friends, and even that's no guarantee.

The sheep pen is close to the house to discourage predators, so when Nuna gets up to do the chores she has to tiptoe around in the dark. If the sheep see her walking around in the kitchen they'll start bleating and wake up everyone.

Ted and Nuna have eclectic interests, reflected in the conversations they have with guests. And since the B&B is only open seasonally, guests who visit Green Hill in May have to beware of Ted, who is a self-described good talker, especially after six months with no guests. "You sit down at the kitchen table," says Nuna, "and whoosh! You're captured!"

Business Definition

A bed and breakfast is typically defined as a business where the owners rent out a small number of rooms in their private home to travelers. The number of rooms can range from one room up through seven, though most bed-and-breakfasts average three or four. In addition to serving breakfast—either a full meal or a simple continental breakfast—a few B&Bs will also provide dinner on occasion to guests, though this is more the exception than the rule.

A bed-and-breakfast differs from an inn, which usually has more rooms and is not considered to be the hosts' private home, though they may live in separate quarters in part of the house.

Revenue from a bed-and-breakfast usually serves as a supplement to the host's income, and one or both of the owners may hold down a full-time job outside the home. I've met hosts who have worked as government consultants, real estate agents, and farmers. Some are retired; many have left their primary careers in their 30s or 40s to start living their dream.

No matter how B&B owners spend their spare time, and there is less of it than you may think, they share one thing in common: they love people and graciously welcome them into their homes.

Running a B&B may be less work overall than a country inn, but with a caveat. An innkeeper with a full staff can concentrate on running the show and doing only the tasks that they want to do. Because a bed-and-breakfast is smaller and usually charges less than an inn, most, if not all, of the work—the good and the bad—falls to the host. From greeting guests to cleaning toilets and chopping vegetables, you should be prepared to do it all. But some people like being in charge of everything and not relying on staff. Even though you'll do most of the work, you still may need to have at least one person on a part-time basis. Chapter 6 will show you how.

There is a hybrid of the B&B and country inn called the B&B inn, which tends to have more rooms than a B&B. Like a country inn, the hosts of a B&B inn live in separate quarters; in a B&B, the owners' room is usually just another bedroom on the same floor as the guest rooms. B&B guests share the owner's house; a B&B inn tends to be more formal.

A B&B can be in the country, the city, or the suburbs. I've stayed in B&Bs in a suburban ranch home, and also a 200-year-old farmhouse that looked as though it hadn't been renovated or decorated in all those years. You may decide to rent out the bedroom of your daughter who's gone to college—and who still comes home at holiday time—or you may decide to buy a house for the sole purpose of running a B&B, whether the business already exists or you have to start from scratch.

Running a B&B is a great way to make a living and to see the world while staying put, since guests from all over the planet will come to see you. You should be forewarned, however, there's a lot more to running a B&B than meets the eye.

Typical Business Day

On your visits to other B&Bs, you've probably sighed and thought, "What a wonderful way to make a living. And doesn't the host look relaxed?"

This first impression of the host is what has been responsible for thousands of people who dream about chucking it all to open a B&B. After all, your life and your job are so stressful that the minute you hang out your B&B sign, you can throw away your high blood pressure medication and...

Not so fast. The times you've chatted with your B&B host on past visits are probably the calmest moments of her day. Many hosts, in fact, regard the task of greeting and spending time with guests as their downtime. The rest of the time, they're probably constantly on the go.

Here's a typical day in front of and behind the scenes for the owner of a B&B. Just for fun, we'll put you in the starring role, Reality, while the guests live your previous image of the B&B, Fantasy.

What The Guest Sees (The Fantasy): 8 A.M.: Guests sit down to a relaxing full breakfast while you take their orders, fill coffee cups, and serve the meal. The guests linger for more than an hour.

What You See (The Reality): 6 A.M.: The alarm goes off. You make a pot of coffee, set the tables, and start preparing the meal. You gave up making fancy garnishes in the first month since they took twice as long to make as the meal itself. The first guests start to filter down the stairs at 7:30, and you make another pot of coffee.

Fantasy: 9:15 A.M.: The last guests leave the breakfast table and announce they are going for a long walk before checkout time.

Reality: 9:16 A.M.: You clear the tables and put the dishes in the dishwasher, and completely clean the kitchen.

Fantasy: 11 A.M.: The guests return from their walk to pack and settle with you for checkout.

Reality: 11 A.M.: You welcome the opportunity to stand in one place for a few minutes and chat with your guests, since you've spent the last 74 minutes answering the phone, telling new early arrivals that they can't check into their room until you clean it—which you hadn't planned to do until the afternoon—and making up your shopping list because you ran out of eggs this morning.

Fantasy: 12 noon: With a final longing look at your B&B, the last guests drive off after making reservations to come back for a weekend in another month.

Reality: 12:01 P.M.: You start to clean the rooms for the new guests and long for summer, when an increasing number of bookings and school vacation mean you can hire a student to make up the rooms every morning.

Fantasy: 1 P.M.: The new guests check into the room.

Reality: 1:15 P.M.: When your guest are settled, you sit down in your office to start to tackle the other work you do. You try to read a pile of newsletters, association news, bills, and letters from guidebooks exhorting you to spend your hard-earned dollars with them for a listing.

Fantasy: 1:15 P.M.: Other guests you're expecting call to say they'll be arriving at nine tonight.

Reality: 1:15 P.M.: There go your plans to go to bed early, but at least it means you can spend a couple of hours out doing errands later this afternoon, thanks to the answering machine.

Fantasy: 2 P.M.: Your new guests tell you they're heading out to sightsee and ask if there any good restaurants around.

Reality: 2 P.M.: You spend the next three hours doing paperwork, only to be interrupted seven times by the phone and pausing to take down addresses and send out brochures.

5:15 P.M.: You finally make it out of the house, but the bank and post office just closed, and so all you can do is go to the supermarket. Fresh, expensive, out-of-season strawberries are just in, but they look so good that you buy them, knowing your guests will love them with cream tomorrow morning. On your way home, you see that your friend Rose—who also runs a B&B—is home, but there are several cars with out-of-state plates in her driveway, and you figure she must be busy so you head home.

Fantasy: 7 P.M.: Your new guests arrive early just as you pull in the driveway. You welcome them inside and show them to their room, which is the most expensive one and the only with a view of the mountains. On your way past your office, you notice that the message light on your answering machine is blinking wildly.

7:10 P.M. The new guests get settled and then leave for dinner.

Reality: 7:10 P.M.: You bring the bags of groceries into the house and unpack them. On your way to check the phone messages, the new guests stop you. The three of you proceed to talk for 45 minutes before they leave for the local Italian place.

Fantasy: 8 P.M.: Silence. Both sets of guests are out.

Reality: 8 P.M.: You sit in the kitchen and grab a quick dinner as you go through the mail and leaf through the paper from this morning.

Fantasy: 9 P.M.: The first couple returns from dinner.

Reality: 9 P.M.: You sit in the living room and offer them wine. You sit and talk.

Fantasy: 9:30 P.M.: The second couple returns.

Reality: 9:31 P.M.: More wine glasses come out.

Fantasy: 10:45 P.M.: The two couples stay up chatting.

Reality: 10:45 P.M.: You look at your watch and yawn before announcing you have to go to sleep "If you don't want me to make your breakfast in my sleep tomorrow."

11 P.M.: You collapse in bed, forgetting all about checking the answering machine.

This is not a negative depiction of what running a B&B is like, but rather a realistic picture. Some people prefer a block of time where they can do their work each day, after which they can forget it exists and leave it back at the office.

Not so with a B&B. First, you're living and working in the same place, so the boundaries can't help but bleed together. Second, it's your business, and you're responsible for its success or failure.

After all, that's what running your own business is all about.

Current Business Environment

In the early '80s, for all intents and purposes the B&B industry as we know it today simply did not exist in this country. B&Bs have long been popular throughout Europe, where the concept first developed after World War II.

As cost-conscious Americans traveled to Europe and stayed in private homes for much less than a hotel would cost, they returned to the States, and the closest thing they could find to a B&B was a country inn.

As country inns grew popular in the '80s and more Americans traveled to Europe, the demand for B&Bs in this country grew. Some of these travelers opened B&Bs of their own because they were so enamored of the ones they experienced overseas. Others also liked the concept and they needed additional income but eschewed full-time boarders or tenants. Still others who had worked in the inn or hotel business wanted to scale down yet stay in the same field.

In areas that pull in tourists who stay for a few days, or in those places where travelers are just passing through, B&Bs are growing in great numbers—especially if there are certain times of the year when every room within a 25-mile radius is booked for a special event like an antiques show or a popular weekend at a racetrack. A new hotel would help absorb the overflow at these times, but would lose money the rest of the year; so B&Bs are a much wiser choice for the local economy as a whole.

Today, California and New York are the states with the most B&B establishments—New York alone has 1,500. It's estimated that there are 25,000 B&B establishments throughout the country. Some country inns call themselves B&Bs—which they technically are if they offer a *bed* and *breakfast*—in order to attract the traveler who is looking to stay in a private home. In these cases of misrepresentation, guests are often disappointed, and word eventually gets out.

The Annual Directory of American and Canadian Bed & Breakfasts (Rutledge Hill Press) is a fat book of B&B listings, with more than 6,000 establishments described. However, the book only includes those B&Bs that are willing to pay $35 to be listed in the book. This fee, as you'll discover, is a common practice in getting the word out about your B&B, at least in the popular guidebooks. Undoubtedly, there are many more B&Bs that are unlicensed, seasonal operations, which tourists turn to only when all known accommodations are taken. For instance, a friend with a house in Barnard, Vermont, one town north of Woodstock, will get a call from the Woodstock Chamber of Commerce for several weekends during foliage season when every room in the state is taken and has been for months. People actually arrive in town without reservations during the busiest time of the year. The Chamber calls her. She sleeps downstairs on the couch, cooks breakfast for the guests in the morning, makes a few new friends, and pockets $100 for the effort. This temporary, very seasonal operation, too, is technically a B&B.

But it is the exception. If you plan to run a B&B as a thriving business, you'll have to get licensed, undergo health and other safety inspections, and be aggressive about marketing your business. But all that comes later. Even with 25,000 known B&Bs in operation in the country today, the market is far from saturated.

You're looking at an industry with great growth potential. Typically, however, the total share of room nights constituted by B&Bs ranges from less than one percent to three percent at the most, when hotels, motels, inns, and other lodging businesses are figured into the equation. But as more travelers begin to search out this unique lodging opportunity, it undoubtedly means increased business for you.

Primary Product

Basically, you are selling two things to your customers: a bed, and a morning meal. But really it amounts to much more than just that, since a traveler can get these things anywhere. Your customers are looking for a unique experience to go along with the basic necessities. They don't want to stay in a large chain hotel, where they'll be just another guest with a room key.

Guests choose a B&B because they eschew the forced formality that is an accepted part of a stay in a chain hotel. They want the intimacy of staying in a private home as well as the chance to get to know an area through the eyes of a person who actually lives there.

And this makes a big difference. In a chain hotel, if you ask staff members for recommendations on what to see or where to eat, they'll probably run down a list of the usual tourist-only haunts in town, probably because the concierge and desk clerk don't want their favorite haunts to be overrun with out-of-towners. With a B&B host, you'll likely hear about places that tourists who stay in chain hotels don't get to hear about.

Not every tourist wants the unavoidable intimacy of a B&B. But, especially in big cities, B&Bs are generally considered to be safer than big-city hotels with long, deserted hallways and stairways. Therefore, many businesswomen traveling alone will choose a B&B primarily for this feature. If unfamiliar with the camaraderie that naturally develops in a B&B, she may initially shun any contact with other guests as well as her hosts. But it probably won't last. The genuine friendliness coming from both guests and hosts at a B&B is contagious, and a woman who chooses to stay at your B&B will leave with feelings she didn't expect—and feelings that she'll return for.

Related Products and Services

Though the B&B will be the primary product you're selling, there are other items and services that you can make available to your guests. While you certainly can consider guests to be a captive audience, you don't want to be too pushy about about the extras you offer. Save your pushiness for marketing your B&B (See Chapter 7).

If you make a special food that will hold up well to travel, like jam, breads, or cookies, you can package and sell it to guests in the common area of your B&B, near where they check in and out. For additional income, many B&Bs also make it a habit to sell guidebooks in which they've been written up—this can also help to boost local tourism. And if you dabble in antiques or arts and crafts, you can let your guests know that the painting hanging on the wall or the small basket filled with potpourri is for sale. It's best to have a separate room for displaying antiques and other large items, if possible. This helps avoid the appearance of desperation that *everything* in the B&B is for sale. You can also offer extra services to your guests, such as breakfast in bed, or dinner or a box lunch for a fee if you're given plenty of notice.

Over time, you'll find that guests will ask about items and services that you didn't even know existed. That's when it helps to belong to the local chamber of commerce or tourism association; if a guest asks where the nearest equestrian center is, or for the name of the best massage therapist in town, you'll know who to call. And if you don't know, stall while you find someone who does.

B&B Niches

Most tourists traveling for pleasure select a B&B based on two criteria: its location, and the feeling conveyed in promotional literature and over the phone.

If you decide to start your B&B in your current house, your location and to some extent your particular niche are limited. The only change you can make is decor, but there again, the structure of the building itself will limit your choices. After all, you don't want to bill yourself as a modern B&B in a house that's 200 years old .

A majority of B&B guests are looking for a sense of history when they choose a B&B. Witness the proliferation of B&Bs with Victorian or Historic in the name, or the year that the house was built. The five most common niches that a B&B can fill are outlined on page 14. Some B&Bs can fall into more than one category.

How Your Lifestyle Will Change

Go back and read the earlier section, "Typical Business Day." Unless you've already been running a boarding house, life as you know it will cease to exist once you get your B&B up and running. One comment that is universal among any kind of small lodging operator is that you should expect to spend a great deal of your time at home. When you have guests, you can't really leave the house. When you're expecting guests to arrive, you should be there to greet them, which can be frustrating when guests arrive late or not at all.

But most B&B owners are able to view their homebound status with a positive twist: the world comes to them. It's true, all kinds of people from all over the world will come to stay with you, and you'll learn about people and places you've never come into contact with before. And for the most part, most of your guests will be on their best behavior, which makes serving them a pleasure.

You'll most likely begin long friendships with your guests, who often invite B&B hosts to stay with them if ever visiting their town. This isn't surprising, however, when you consider that travelers who choose to stay in B&Bs are specifically looking for that kind of personal contact.

1. **Historic:** The pull here is that guests can feel like they're traveling back in time to a less hurried world.

2. **Utilitarian:** Here, decor is downplayed. As a result the B&B itself is nothing special. But this type of B&B frequently emerges when empty nesters decide to put a couple of spare rooms to use. Usually the furniture stays the same, the rock-star posters in the kids' bedrooms come down, and a stack of fresh towels goes on the bureau.

3. **Farm:** In the summer of 1993, I stayed at more than 40 B&Bs while researching a book on farm vacations in New England. I met some of the most informal and warmest hosts in the business. A farm B&B is distinctive because the hosts operate an agricultural business that may consist of 40 acres of corn, or a few sheep and a small garden plot where the crops are sold at a roadside stand. Guests are welcome to help with the chores, and often do, but depending upon the size of the farm, the animals or crops come first, which most guests understand and respect.

4. **City B&B:** This might be an extra room in a two-bedroom city apartment or a suite in a sprawling townhouse. City B&Bs are usually located in safe neighborhoods and tend to be near major attractions or business districts.

5. **Separate Dwelling:** I once stayed in a four-room cabin next to a house with four other B&B rooms. My cabin had a fully-furnished kitchen, and when I woke in the morning the table was set, coffee was brewing, and pancake batter mixed and ready to go. Other times hosts with a separate dwelling just provide the fixings and leave the preparation to the guests or invite them inside when there are other guests.

If you've never worked at home or for yourself before, be prepared for a big surprise: the business will do its best to spill over into every corner of your life—that is, if you let it. That's why every B&B host who's been in the business for a while makes it a point to get away from the house for fun at least once a week, even if they have to hire someone to babysit the B&B for an evening.

If you are seriously considering opening a B&B, you must carefully evaluate your housekeeping habits. Guests expect uncluttered and clean spaces when they travel. Look at Holiday Inn: What would you think about the owners if you found crumbs or a dirty sink when you checked into your room? Many guests will not give exact reasons, but if they check out almost immediately after you've shown them to their rooms, the chances are they found the cleanliness to be not up to their standards.

You may be all gung-ho about opening a B&B, but consider the other members of your family and how they might feel. If you have a teenage daughter, I'd bet that she wouldn't appreciate the lack of privacy and the prospect of facing strangers across the breakfast table every morning. A younger child might enjoy the constant influx of guests, as well as a particular role in the operation of the B&B, such as Official Greeter entertaining guests' children and showing them around.

You should be sure your spouse is in total agreement with your plans. While you may be doing most of the work, the fact is that he or she may be asked to pitch in every so often. I once visited a B&B where I had made my reservation with the wife, who ran the business. But it was the husband who came out and barked at me when I arrived and parked in the wrong space. This tempered my experience at this B&B, even though other aspects of the place were well above average. So if even one person in your household is opposed to the idea, you should work out your differences before you begin to plan your B&B. Play it safe. Before you proceed with your plans, be sure you sit down with all family members to get their feedback.

As for cooking, though you don't have to be trained at the Culinary Institute of America, you do need some basic cooking and presentation skills. Think of how your food looks when you eat out. B&B guests don't necessarily expect gourmet cuisine, but they do want good food that's skillfully prepared, and enough of it. Some B&B owners skip the cooking and instead offer an easy-to-fix continental breakfast of breads and pastries, coffee and juice. Indeed, some health departments forbid establishments in private homes from serving a hot meal to guests. You should check with the department before you decide on your menu.

In the end, if you love people and want to share your house and the area in which you live, you'll make a great B&B host.

Income and Profit Potential

As with any business, in the beginning it may seem as though you're working for free, as you pour every penny of revenue back into the B&B, whether buying a piano for the living room, a bread maker for the kitchen, or more ads or brochures.

Don't worry. Though a B&B is a business that can tie up a significant amount of cash in the beginning, if you keep your expenses down while increasing your occupancy rate with inexpensive marketing techniques (see Chapter 7), in time you'll be able to breathe easier and pay yourself a salary as well.

The amount of money you'll be able to eventually realize depends on the number of rooms in your B&B, the rates you charge, and your occupancy rate. Some B&Bs with only two or three rooms that rent for $40 a night and are primarily booked during the summer season will only pull in a few thousand dollars of revenue over the course of a year. But some hosts who have the extra space anyway keep the B&B as a sideline business and see the income as pure profit. Expenses for utilities in the summertime are usually negligible.

However, most B&B owners do want their rooms to generate significant income, so they aggressively promote the B&B and upgrade the tone and decor of their home to justify charging $100 a night or more. It all depends on the kind of business you'd like to run.

What matters most when it comes to success is your attitude towards the business and towards the guests. Repeat business is the lifeblood of the lodging industry, and if guests enjoy their stay at your B&B and spending time with you, they'll come back, and they'll tell their friends about you.

Risk Potential

Any business that relies on tourists is going to have some months that are insanely busy, while in others you'll be lucky to fill one room on the weekend. If you don't plan for these fluctuations and budget your money accordingly, you will run into problems, especially if you bought the B&B or a house to convert. There are a number of creative promotions to increase your off-season business, but nothing can totally make up for the slow seasons, which are usually dependent on the weather.

Location is another important factor in determining whether or not you will succeed. B&Bs located in areas where tourists seldom venture are more likely to fall into the category of a hobby business. If you open a B&B in a popular tourist area, the odds of making it are better, though it is usually more expensive to run the business.

I know of an inn and B&B consultant who advised a couple against buying a B&B in a particular town "because no one ever drives through it." True, the couple could have made it work with a lot of sweat and determination, but if people are already coming to an area for its specific attractions, and your B&B just happens to be nearby, a lot of the marketing work is already done for you, usually by the state tourism bureau and the local chamber of commerce.

Action Guidelines

✔ Realize that B&B is a bona fide business, where you'll probably work harder than ever before.

✔ B&Bs will only grow in popularity as a travel option through the end of the decade and into the next.

✔ Consider what type of niche you'd like your B&B to fill.

✔ Talk candidly with your family about how the B&B will change your lives.

✔ Expect some risk; the hospitality field can be a highly volatile, very seasonal business.

✔ Be prepared to send out hundreds more Christmas cards each year as guests become lifelong friends.

$$B\&B\ Profile$$

Mary Lalumiere
Mari's Bed & Breakfast
Cumberland, Maine

When guests walk in the front door of Mari's Bed & Breakfast, located in a quiet bedroom community of Portland, Maine, the first thing that owner Mary Lalumiere does is ask if they've eaten dinner, or if they want some cookies or need to do laundry. This kind of hospitality is present every minute of a guest's visit at Mari's, a comfortable five-bedroom Victorian farmhouse built in 1898. Many guests return again and again, just to see Mary; indeed, some say it's like going back to an aunt's or a grandmother's house as an adult.

There are several sitting rooms downstairs, a big front porch, and even an built-in swimming pool in the backyard. Mary's 15 acres contain marigolds, buttercups, roses, thistle, clover, daisies, and juniper that she specially cultivates to incorporate into the more than four thousand pieces of pottery she makes in her basement every year. She gives guests a piece of pottery when they leave.

In addition to the B&B and her pottery business, Mary works part-time as a nurse. Unlike many busy people, however, when she sits down to talk with guests she makes it seem as though she has all the time in the world.

"I run the bed and breakfast like a family," she says, adding that she comes from a family of five and lived on a farm with a guesthouse that had seven rooms, so she's used to having lots of people around.

"In the B&B business, you have to come across that you're not afraid of people, and that most people are basically good," she says. "One time I had 11 guests and 13 people at breakfast, and we hung around the dining room table and went through five pots of coffee by the time we were done. It was 11 A.M. when everybody left and I went back to work, but it was great, I loved every minute of it."

That effervescence was what attracted her into the bed and breakfast business in the first place. In 1987, a local real estate agent asked Mary if she would take in a family who was moving to the area. Their house in Illinois had sold more quickly than they had anticipated. The family of four moved in for four months. Mary saw it as a testing ground for the B&B, which officially opened in 1988. Ever since, half of her business has been guests who have been to Mari's at least twice.

REQUIREMENTS

Before you proceed to plan your B&B, it's a good idea to take some time to evaluate yourself, your financial situation, and the house you plan to use for your B&B. Doing your homework at this stage will save you from making big and possibly costly mistakes down the road.

Assessing Your Personal Goals

First, you must determine what your overall personal goals are and how owning a B&B fits with them.

Take some time to answer the following questions in detail:

- What are the three main reasons why you want to open a B&B?
- Why do you want to run a business that involves a lot of social interaction from your home?
- How long to you plan to run the B&B?
- Do you see the B&B as a hobby or as a full-time business?
- What are your personal goals aside from the B&B? Do you plan to retire at a certain age, or move on to something else after running the business for ten years?

Some people decide to open a B&B because they have a few spare rooms that could be earning some money, while others opt for the business because they've stayed at countless B&Bs on vacation and have fantasized being in the hosts' shoes.

As you've seen in Chapter One, the fantasy does not even begin to match the reality—even though you won't fully admit to this until you're knee-deep in the business. Many prospective B&B hosts view the business as a means to an end: This is a way they can go into semi- or early retirement; or the only way they can finally move to the country and be able to make a living. Empty-nesters, who no longer have children living at home, not only see the kids' bedrooms as potential income generators, but more than a few are surprised that the guests are a welcome replacement for the quiet they discovered they didn't want after all.

Other people dream of the self-sufficiency of running their own business. Certainly homebodies who want their houses to generate some income and allow them to live off the land will appeal to many who want to get away from it all without losing contact with other people.

One New Hampshire couple started their three-room B&B after their kids and a variety of foreign exchange students went off to college. They plan to run the business for five to seven years, and then either close it or sell it so they can spend some time traveling around the country in an RV. However, most people who start a B&B see it as a long-term venture.

If you like the idea of hosting house guests who pay you to stay in your house, but you want to be able to hang out a No Vacancy sign when you don't want to see another human being for awhile, it's possible to do so without guilt if you regard the B&B as a part-time pursuit or a supplement to your other activities. Larger B&Bs that serve as the hosts' sole source of income can also close up shop for a few days, but because they rely more on the income than hobby B&B hosts do, they might be hesitant about doing this during peak season and may instead wait until a slow time of year.

A B&B is like any other business: It must provide income along with a healthy dose of satisfaction. You also need to have something in your life besides the business. That's why it's important to set goals for yourself that are totally separate from the business. Burn-out is very common when you run a B&B, and one way to prevent it is to plan your goals in advance, whether you want to learn a foreign language or spend more time with your friends and family. In this business, leisure is both possible and very necessary.

Assessing Your Personal Values

Some people would make terrible B&B hosts because they can't stand the idea of being in service to another person.

Then there are those people who consider it a sign of respect to offer people a bed in their home, serve them a meal, and spend quiet time in conversation. To evaluate whether your personal values mesh with running a B&B, ask yourself the following questions:

- Do you enjoy making people happy with the things you can do for them, more than the things you can give them? If you answered yes, give an example.

- Are you a stickler when it comes to cleanliness and punctuality—your own, not your guests?

- Are you usually able to see the good in people, especially when their values are the opposite of yours?

- How patient are you?

It may seem as if you need the demeanor of Gandhi to run a B&B, since you will be dealing with many different kinds of people. However, if you consider your tolerance level to be above that of the general population and you have the desire—or discipline—to have your guests come first, then you'll be an excellent B&B host. Keep in mind that you won't have a year-round 100 percent occupancy rate, so you will have down times when you can relax, go out, and be served.

If you're the type of person who always has to be right, even if you excel at biting your tongue at strategic moments, guests can tell. Although altercations between hosts and guests are extremely rare, I know of at least one host who asked a guest to leave because her hostility was affecting the other guests. Even though she had already spent one night at the B&B, the host wrote her out a check for the full amount that she had paid and politely asked her to check out several days early.

The best B&B hosts are patient, genuinely curious about different types of people, and are able to shrug things off. I once stayed in a luxurious B&B where the bed was so comfortable I had a hard time getting up. As a result, I was 15 minutes late for breakfast, and as soon as I got downstairs the host snapped at me and practically threw my breakfast on the table. I found out much later that he held a full-time job and because I was late, he would be late. But whenever I think of that B&B, I remember that incident, and not the bed.

As a B&B host you should learn to let the little things slide—because there certainly will be plenty of them.

Assessing Your Financial Goals

If you want to get rich, go buy a book by Charles Givens. If you want to have a decent income while you build equity and increase your revenues a little bit each year, then keep reading. To see if your financial goals jive with running a B&B, ask yourself the following questions:

- What would you rather have after ten years of hard work: A large sum of money in the bank, or equity in a valuable home and business that would be relatively easy to sell?

- What's the least amount of money you could live on each month, provided that the mortgage, taxes, and utilities are paid for?
- Do you like doing just one thing to make a living, or do you prefer to juggle a variety of tasks?

For most people who decide to open a B&B, money is of secondary concern. Of course, it takes money to get started whether you have one room or ten, but most people are looking for the lifestyle first and income second. These priorities will help keep you motivated during the slow times.

After the uncertainties of the first year that you're up and running, it will seem like you can relax a little as room revenue becomes a bit more predictable, but you'll still find it necessary to reinvest much of the money back into the business in order to keep your revenue growing. Because of this, unless you have a trust fund or a sizable side income, you must learn to live frugally and get used to the idea of being house-rich but cash-poor, at least for awhile. In time, most B&B owners learn to see this aspect of the business as a benefit, as the B&B and the guests provide them with priceless knowledge and experience that they couldn't get any other way.

In many cases the occupancy rate in a city B&B tends to be higher and steadier than at a rural B&B; urban B&Bs rely more on business people, who travel no matter what the season. Urban tourism also seems to be steadier.

Travelers to rural areas, on the other hand, have definite seasons that they like to travel, whether it's ski season, summer, or foliage. As a result, while you can predict your busy periods, it may be difficult to stretch the money out over slow times. You may need to do other things to carry you over until business picks up again—and it will. This may mean developing ancillary products and services to sell to your guests, starting a sideline business, or even getting an outside job. Even though you may be working twice as hard running a B&B as anything you've done before, most B&B owners say they wouldn't trade it for any amount of money.

Assessing Your Risk Tolerance

Many people who dream of opening a B&B love the idea and constantly fantasize about it, but when it comes right down to it, most will never take the necessary steps because they're reluctant to leave the security of having a regular job, health insurance, the familiarity of a particular lifestyle—you name it—even if they're unhappy in their current lives. A person who falls into this category has a low tolerance for risk of any kind.

On the other hand, people who can tolerate risk, even welcome it to some degree, recognize that even though they may do everything necessary to operate and promote the business successfully, there is still some element of risk to the business beyond their control, like economic downturns and fickle weather. They accept this as a normal part of doing business, and proceed accordingly.

What's your tolerance for risk? Find out by answering the following questions:

- Have you ever run a business of your own before? If so, how did you react when things slowed down? If you don't have experience in running a business, how do you think you would react—with panic, or the ability to constantly keep the big picture in mind?
- How would you react if business was slow and you didn't have enough money to pay the mortgage?
- How important is it to you to have material items to validate your self-worth? What would you do if you were to suddenly lose them?

People who don't have a high tolerance for risky situations often see the world in black and white, with no room for gray areas. Sure, the prospect of quitting your job and opening a B&B, maybe even moving to a new area, is frightening even to people who like some excitement. There's no safety net; what makes me think I can pull this off; and what if I fail? are probably only three of the concerns that are running through your head before you decide to start your B&B. However, men and women who are able to see these factors as challenges to meet and surpass, and who like the absence of a schedule—as well as not knowing what the next day or week will bring—should be able to deal well with the unpredictable nature of the business.

And sometimes, in order to get into the business, it's necessary to do without the things you treasure. Many people finance their B&B by selling family heirlooms, cars, even their homes, when there's no guarantee they'll be able to succeed. If you place great importance on your possessions and hate the idea of essentially gambling with their value, you should think twice about spending a lot of money to open your B&B, or else find someone else to finance it.

Tools and Equipment

The most important tool for a B&B is the house where guests will stay. You will need to evaluate it with a critical eye to determine if it meets the standards to which guests are accustomed, or if you'll need to make some changes.

Because you're thinking about opening a B&B, you've probably visited others in the past. Now, it's a good idea to take the time to visit them again as you plan your own. Select five other B&Bs in your area and visit them as a guest. As you visit, ask yourself the following questions:

- What do you like about them?
- What don't you like?
- How is each one different from the others?
- In your opinion, what can improve the physical appearance and tone of each one?
- Is there anything that seems out of place at any of them?
- What are the five things that you look for when you decide to stay at a B&B? Since every B&B reflects the

tastes and desires of its owners, this list will help you to model your own home into a successful B&B.

When you get home, take notes on each one. Which characteristics that you saw would you like to incorporate into your own B&B? What could you do to make your B&B different from the others? For this last question, spend some time thinking about it, because what makes your B&B unique and sets it apart from the others in your area will help later when it comes time to market your B&B.

It's also important to analyze the physical layout of your house—or of the house or B&B you're buying—and determine if the space is suitable for the type for B&B you want to operate. For instance, if you have three empty rooms or less, your business will probably be only a sideline. With four or more rooms, you will be spending more time on the business and will probably need to hire staff from time to time. Do you really want to do this? Even if you have five spare rooms to rent out, it may be a good idea to fix up only two or three at first as a way to test yourself for the business. You can always expand later.

What do the common areas of your home feel like? Will people want to spend time relaxing in them? Remember, guests are not going to spend all their time in their rooms; they'll want the equivalent of a living room where they can read, watch TV, or mingle with you and the other guests. If the doors to certain rooms are open, guests are going to assume they can go into them. At one B&B, I walked from the living room into a room off the side through an open door. The host immediately stopped me and said, "That's not public space." I didn't say anything, but I thought if it was a private space that they should at least close the door.

Finally, analyze your furniture and make a list of the pieces you'll have to buy, either new or at a second-hand store. You can probably get anything you need used and save a lot of money, except for towels and linens. Threadbare towels and faded, worn bedsheets and blankets will do more than anything else to turn guests off. Some of them will assume that your same lack of attention extends to cleanliness and hygiene, so spend as much as you can on linens and towels for guests.

Take a look at your kitchen and your cooking equipment, dishes, serving utensils, and platters. A commercial coffee maker or two household coffee makers are essential when some guests drink regular and others prefer decaf. Do you have enough pans to make six omelets in a row without having to stop and wash them?

In a B&B, guests don't seem to be as picky about the place settings and utensils, because, after all, they realize they are staying in someone's home. So you don't have to be concerned about having everything match, though some hosts do go all out for breakfast, with crystal and china.

In the dining room, the guests usually eat at one table, so it should be large enough to accommodate the number of guests when your rooms are filled to capacity. Even so, some mornings you'll find you need more; perhaps the children of guests are staying over—that is, if you allow children—or a guest asks friends in the area to join them at breakfast. Be sure that you have a couple of smaller tables for the overflow.

You'll also need a telephone for guests, an outside line that allows them to make free local calls but requires a calling card for long-distance calls. Or else you can arrange with the telephone company to install a pay phone.

Up until 1993, most B&Bs didn't provide locks on guest room doors because they operated on a system of trust. More people now are interested in security, and one of the biggest guidebooks ruled in 1993 that it wouldn't list B&Bs that didn't have locks on the doors. Though many rooms have sliding bolts that guests can operate from the inside of the room, a number of B&B owners still prefer to not put locks on the doors. It's your call.

You should also evaluate your bathrooms. Though most travelers are accustomed to having a private bath in their room from years of staying in chain hotels, some guests will accept the inconvenience of a shared bath in exchange for a cheaper room rate. Analyze each bath that guests will be using, and use common sense to determine what needs attention and what could be left alone. Most of the improvements can be done cheaply, from replacing floor tiles to fixing leaks or cleaning stubborn rust stains. Remember, it doesn't have to be perfect, but it should be in keeping with the character of the rest of your house.

Most people prefer a firm mattress, so if any of the mattresses on your guest beds sag in the middle, you must replace them. Some guests with back problems may ask if you have bed boards for added firmness, so it pays to invest in this as well.

Undoubtedly, if you have more than one guest room, you will be able to rate them in terms of comfort, attractiveness, and size. Many B&B hosts routinely book their smallest rooms last, only if all of the others fill up. And they make this fact clear to the person on the phone who is reserving the room, who will probably not notice its size upon arrival because she hasn't had anything to compare it to. The hosts may then automatically move them up to a nicer room at the small-room price when a vacancy occurs. But sometimes they won't. At one B&B, the host put me in a small room that shared a wall with a larger room. A couple and their 12-year-old son stayed in that room the night I was there, and they made so much noise late at night and early in the morning that I didn't sleep well. I didn't understand why the hosts didn't put me in a room across the hall that was more private and cost the same. They may have figured that two rooms that were close together would have made housekeeping easier the next morning, but it only served to alienate me. Unfortunately, the hosts were out all night, so I couldn't ask if I could move to that room.

And check your laundry facilities: If you'll need to do five loads a day when you're fully booked, either upgrade the capacity of your washer and dryer, or have plenty of spare linens and towels on hand so you don't have to spend your entire day doing laundry.

There are some modifications that will be mandated by licenses and permits (see Chapter 5) such as the number of parking spaces, smoke detectors, or fire exits.

Financial Requirements

The cost of opening a B&B can vary widely, depending upon the vision you have of your B&B and whether you can open it in your present home or need a bigger house. The price of buying an existing B&B will always be more than buying a similar house in the same area and then converting it. If the price seems ridiculously low, then you're right to be suspicious since you're buying a going business supposedly with a built-in customer list and a good reputation. Starting from scratch means less revenue in the beginning, but also less expense to get started. Cheapest of all is to set up a B&B in your present house—if it's appropriate.

No matter how you start, however, you will need to invest a sizable amount of money not only in physically setting up your B&B, but also for permits, licenses, and insurance. I hesitate to give exact figures for expenses, since I know there are people out there who have spent much less and also those who splurged. But what follows is a general range.

If you are opening a B&B in your home, you should plan on spending at least $500 to $1,000 per room to spruce up the guest rooms and the house (not including the cost of any furniture) as well as setting up the business. Furnishing each room from scratch could run another $500 to $1,000 and up per room if you shop at secondhand stores.

Several factors influence the cost of an existing B&B: Location, size, and style (whether opulent with lots of extras or a low-budget operation). In a prime tourist area, a B&B with four or five guest rooms can start at $125,000 and go up from there. However, it's been my experience that people who can afford much more than that tend to buy an inn rather than a B&B, so the most you'd expect to pay for a B&B is somewhere around $300,000.

If you start from scratch, the amount you'll need to get the business up and running includes the house itself, furniture for the rooms and common areas, decor, and licenses, insurance and other fees. In some parts of the country it's possible to spend under $100,000 for an older house with four or five bedrooms—don't forget to reserve one for yourself—but in that price range you may need to invest so much money in the structure or major systems like heating and plumbing that by the time you're ready to open, you probably could have bought an existing B&B for what you've spent.

Because many people are eager to start their businesses right away, they choose to spend more money at the outset so they can start making money right away. If you have the patience and the cash to fix up what may turn out to be a money pit, then take your time—at least you'll have a place to live while you bring your dream to fruition.

Skill Requirements

Many prospective B&B hosts take a variety of seminars, work with consultants, and talk to countless other B&B owners to get an idea of what it's like to run a B&B and all they need to know. No matter how well you prepare, once your first guest arrives and you try in vain to hide your nervousness, you will call many different skills into play.

As stated, the most important skill you'll need is knowing how to deal with people. Without a genuine love for and curiosity about people it's doubtful you'll be able to succeed in the business. After all, when guests tell why they return to a particular B&B, most often they say it's the hosts and the feeling that they were part of the family.

Other skills that you'll need fall under the category of running a business, which any new entrepreneur can learn about from the variety of books on how to start a business. You'll need to learn about cash flow, bookkeeping, and marketing; but again you can usually learn as you go and also by asking other B&B owners what business methods have worked best for them.

Even if you've never run a business before, you probably already know your strengths from working for other people. And where your skills aren't as good, you'll be able to learn enough to get by. If you can afford to hire someone else to do the work, however, go ahead.

Attitude Requirements

The ideal person to run a B&B is a cynical optimist, or, as some might say, an optimistic cynic. This is a person who has a positive attitude towards the world but is not surprised when things go wrong. When that happens, you spring into action and do whatever it takes to address the problem and get everything back to normal—until the next breakdown, that is.

Because as a B&B host you'll be dealing with a variety of people as well as a business, in essence, operating 24 hours a day, surprises will come up from time to time, especially in the beginning. As long as you maintain a positive attitude and remain alert to problems that need your immediate attention while learning patience for those that can wait, you'll be able to run a successful B&B and keep your equilibrium as well. And remember, at least once a week you should take a few hours to get away from the business—this will help you maintain your positive attitude as well.

Your Assets and Liabilities

Before you start planning your B&B, it's a good idea to analyze your assets and liabilities—personal, financial, and those involving your house.

Starting up any business is rough. A B&B can be especially hard because you will be sharing your home with strangers and living in the same place you work. People who run other types of home-based businesses can usually close the door to their office to take a break, but with a B&B, it virtually takes over your entire house. How will you and your family cope with the adjustment? If you communicate well in your family and plan in advance to share some private downtime together each day, you will keep the true purpose of your B&B in the forefront with the right priorities.

As for the house, whenever real estate is involved experts always say you should budget at least twice as much as you think you need. And by the way, the same philosophy also applies to the amount of time you'll need to get your business up and running. But in terms of money, you'll need a financial cushion of several thousand dollars at the very least, and much more than that is recommended. There are always extra expenses for which you haven't budgeted, and some emergencies will require an immediate infusion of cash. Most often this will involve the house itself—maybe you forget to order extra firewood and it's late in the season when wood is more expensive, or perhaps the washer breaks down in the middle of a busy weekend and you need to replace it first thing Monday morning. Your liabilities can be addressed quickly if you have the assets—that is, the extra cash—to fix them as soon as possible

Using Technology to Succeed

It's almost impossible to envision what it would be like to run a business without a computer or fax machine, but every so often I find a B&B that still does everything by ink, ledger, and mail. These people are the staunch holdouts in an increasingly technical world. Many new B&B owners wouldn't dream of starting their business without a computer because they've seen how invaluable they are to business in their other jobs.

Specialty software companies now offer programs designed for B&B owners that will help streamline your reservations system. Other vital programs include word processing, a database, and accounting software. If you plan to write and design your own brochure and other promotional materials, there are several good desktop publishing systems that will lead you by the hand through the entire process.

Though both Macintosh and DOS systems have had their day in the spotlight, the popular Windows system is both user friendly and offers access to many more software programs than are currently available for either Macintosh or DOS. Who knows, at some point in the future you may be corresponding with prospective guests and taking reservations via modem on the Internet, a vast telecommunications system that allows people to send messages to each other via computer.

As for a fax machine, I would say that it's almost necessary equipment for a B&B these days. Not only do many guests make reservations by fax, but the various tourist bureaus and reservation services frequently correspond by fax, whether it's referring a guest or sending late breaking news to their members.

You have several options when setting up a fax machine: you can get a machine with its own dedicated phone line; you can share the fax with your regular telephone line; or you can send and receive faxes through a special modem with your computer. Many people prefer the first option, since both of the others require that you interrupt the use of your phone or computer to accept transmissions. However, it's your choice; computer faxes have the benefit of being able to transmit documents directly from your computer files—you don't even have to print them out first.

Another technological tool you might want to consider is a copier. The personal cartridge copiers will suffice for many B&Bs that don't make a lot of copies. Other than that, the most advanced technological device I've seen a B&B provide for guests was a laser disc player.

Action Guidelines

✔ Take some time to decide if you're right for the business and if the business is right for you.

✔ Evaluate whether the slow and steady financial growth of a B&B matches up with your personal goals.

✔ If you don't have the stomach for risk-taking, lay in a big supply of Maalox if you're determined to open a B&B.

✔ Make a list of the tools and equipment you'll need to open your B&B.

✔ Figure out how much money you'll need to start.

✔ Decide which tasks you'll assume based on your own skills.

✔ Invest in technology to help streamline the operation of your B&B.

⟨ *B&B Profile* ⟩

Francoise Roddy
The Wood's House
Ashland, Oregon

After thinking about the business for ten years, Francoise Roddy and her husband, Lester, pulled up roots from San Francisco's Bay Area and moved to Oregon to open their first B&B. Over the years, the Roddys had stayed at many different B&Bs, joined a B&B trade association and read lots of books about the business.

They settled on Ashland, about 60 miles inland and right off Interstate 5, because the town attracted a steady stream of tourists from February through October for the local Shakespeare festival. They had been looking at a few B&B businesses, and when the real estate agent showed them the Wood's House, Francoise said she walked in and knew this was the B&B that they'd buy. "I knew if we felt that good about it, then our guests would too," she said. "Twelve weeks later we were welcoming our guests."

The Wood's House is a Craftsman inn built in 1908. The Craftsman style differs from its contemporary, Victorian, in that the architecture has a more horizontal orientation. The decor is romantic, with English oak antiques, lots of lace, handprinted wallpaper, and Oriental carpets. "It's very comfortable, but not so full of stuff that you can't feel you're at home," says Francoise.

They chose to buy an existing business because they wanted a B&B that already had a clientele. Plus, they were not interested in doing extensive renovations on a building. "I think people who start from scratch get burned-out sooner because they don't understand how much work is involved and how much time it takes to get known when you're starting at zero," says Francoise. "They think it's going to be a better financial deal because they're paying less for the property, but then they have so much to put in. Today most people want private baths, which cost money to install, and in addition, you have to market the business." She notes that other B&B hosts in Ashland who started their own businesses from scratch usually haven't stayed in the business for more than five years.

The hardest part about the business was learning how to cook breakfast for twelve people at one time. "I arranged it so that part of the sales deal was that the previous owner would spend five days with me teaching me tricks of the trade," she says. For instance, when you're making pancakes, you put them in the oven once they're cooked. Then, when you're ready to serve, you put two on the plate from the oven, and one on top from the griddle. "It's like a little performance every morning, in addition to a challenge," she says.

Her own experience at other B&Bs, plus the stories that her guests tell her, provide ideas to keep refining The Wood's House. "Our guests frequently tell us about some of the B&Bs they've visited, where they've looked lovely on the outside, but the hosts are cold and make the guests feel like they're imposing," she says. "Sometimes, the host will be short with them, and it ruins it. You can be sure the guest won't return."

During her own visits she has awakened in a beautiful, romantic B&B with her husband only to hear a squalling child in the next room. Also, hearing too much of the noise from the kitchen or seeing moldy shower curtains in the bathroom is a guarantee that she won't return.

But the biggest surprise she's had since buying the B&B is what wonderful people her guests are, and the appreciation they show. "It takes so little to make people so happy," she says. "Out in the world today, people are so unnurtured."

The Wood's House has six rooms available for guests; they cost $110 in the high season of summer, while in the winter the price goes down to $65.

After running the B&B for three years, the Roddys found that 80 percent of their guests had stayed there before. "We encourage our return guests," says Francoise. "The purpose of marketing is to let people know what you have. With people who already know us, we can save the education step." Her special promotions include a frequent guest program, which gives guests a third night free in the off-season; a murder mystery weekend; and workshops for aspiring innkeepers. A number of traveling business people stay at The Wood's House after hearing about it from people at local corporations.

To get the word out about the B&B, she donates free weekends to local public TV auctions and advertises her murder mystery weekends. However, she doesn't rely on advertising, believing it a mistake that many B&B hosts make. "Many B&B hosts put money into advertising without first investigating whether it would be worthwhile. Salespeople will call me up several times a month soliciting advertising, but my number one rule is that I don't agree to anything over the phone," she says. She did join the local Ashland B&B network, which puts out a brochure marketing its members. The association has both a local and an 800 number, which members take turns answering on a daily basis. The brochures are distributed at AAA offices, highway information centers, and other businesses around town.

Her advice for aspiring B&B owners is to look at the business thoroughly before you decide to do it. "Take a hands-on workshop, anything where you can find out what the reality of it is," she says. "Many people see it from the guests' perspective, which should appear effortless, which is what we as hosts want it to be. But when it comes to the reality, you'll have some very long days. Often, I'm folding towels at eleven at night. There's more to do than you can see.

"But I don't see it as work, since I enjoy what I'm doing, and I don't feel tied down."

Oh, and one more important piece of advice. "Don't do French toast," says Francoise. "Eighty percent of B&Bs do

French toast, so you should do something different that's fresh and beautifully laid out." Francoise loves to cook, and at The Wood's House she makes griddle cakes with fresh fruit, savory tomato asparagus pie, eggs Romanoff, and cheese blintzes. "We make sure we don't give people the same dish twice."

Chapter
3

RESOURCES

When you start your B&B, you are not alone. Not only is there a wealth of information about the industry and the technical aspects setting up your business, but there are also specific suppliers who specialize in providing B&B owners with the products to truly make their B&B as individual as they are.

Your Own Experiences

When it comes time to utilize the vast array of resources that are available to help you plan your B&B, one of the best ways to begin is through your own experience. You've visited other B&Bs, and you know what they're like and how different they can be.

Perhaps you worked at a summer resort or inn as a teenager—you saw what attracted people to the destination and what kept bringing them back year after year. If your primary expertise is in frequently hosting a house full of friends and relatives, again, you already know about one of the most important parts of the business: treating people like they're your personal houseguests. After all, that's what B&B guests like and appreciate most.

Some people feel that no matter what their experience has been, they need a more formal introduction to the business before they invest a lot of money. So they sign up as hosts and employees at a nearby, established B&B or inn to get a clear picture of what it's like. Some consultants actually advise that if you decide to go this route, you do it during the busiest time of the year. The reasoning? If you can get through this and still want to open your own B&B, then you'll do well in the business.

Researching Customer Needs

Unlike many other businesses, a prospective B&B owner doesn't start out by examining what her customers are looking for. The demand for an intimate stay is there; your customers have already, for the most part, made up their minds that they want to stay in a B&B. What makes them settle on your B&B involves some things that can be measured as well as a few elements that can't.

From the moment a customer receives your brochure to the first time they hear your voice on the phone, a number of factors are influencing their decision about whether or not to make a reservation with you. Some things you can't change, while other, more tangible things, you can.

Private baths, price, and location are some of the factors that enter into the equation. However, as with any business, you can't expect to please everyone who may call or write for a brochure.

The most important way to make your customers happy is to design your B&B in such a way that would make *you* happy. So many of the factors that will influence your customers' decision-making are fixed. The best thing you can do is to make your B&B into the kind of place where you'd feel comfortable staying. Then, undoubtedly, so will your guests.

Trade Associations

Since the number of B&Bs exploded in the early '80s, several trade associations have sprung up to serve the particular needs of B&B owners. Most associations publish a regular newsletter for their members, sell literature on specific aspects of the business, and hold occasional conventions where members can network, attend workshops, and visit trade show exhibitors with products pertinent to the business. Some associations also offer their members consultation services at reduced rates, credit-card acceptance privileges through a clearinghouse, and long-distance and 800 number services at a discount. Though yearly membership rates can be high—up to $150 a year or more—B&B owners report that it's worthwhile because of all the benefits, networking, and ideas they receive.

In addition to the national hospitality and lodging associations, there are many regional, statewide, and local organizations which provide local marketing opportunities. For instance, some of the smaller B&B associations are started by groups of local members of a particular national organization. They meet through the national association, talk regularly on their own, then decide to form their own chapter. Some hosts even start their own associations. For example, there's the Maine Farm Bed & Breakfast Association, a consortium of 15 farms in Maine that take in guests. I've even heard of groups of Victorian or romantic B&Bs that have pooled their resources, hold regular meetings, and even chip in on designing and printing a brochure with a write-up and picture of each member as well as the number of a main contact.

National Associations

The two major national B&B associations are the American Bed & Breakfast Association, or ABBA; and the Professional Association of Innkeepers International, also called PAII.

Both groups offer a regular newsletter and an occasional conference. That's where the similarities end, however. ABBA focuses exclusively on bed and breakfasts, while PAII (pronounced "pie") aims its services towards inns and B&Bs.

ABBA
1407 Huguenot Rd.
Midlothian, VA 23113
804-379-2222

PAII
P.O. Box 90710
Santa Barbara, CA 93190
805-569-1853

You also shouldn't overlook the local, regional and state tourism associations and chambers of commerce for information and networking opportunities in your area.

State Associations

Following is a list of statewide B&B associations. Most are run by the B&B hosts themselves, and the responsibilities frequently revolve among the members. Keep in mind that not every state has a B&B association; in most cases, they've been organized when one or more B&B host has recognized the need for one, as well as its benefits. There are hundreds more that focus on smaller regions, and the state associations will be able to provide you with information on these groups, as can other B&B hosts in your area.

Arizona Association of B&B Inns
3101 N. Central Ave.
Suite 560
Phoenix, AZ 85012
602-274-6302

California Association of B&B Inns
2715 Porter St.
Soquel, CA 95073

B&B Innkeepers of Colorado
1102 W. Pikes Peak Ave.
Colorado Springs, CO 80904
719-471-3980

B&B Inns of Connecticut
35 Hayward Ave.
Colchester, CT 06415
203-537-5772

Georgia B&B Council
600 W. Peachtree St.
Suite 1500
Atlanta, GA 30308
404-873-4482

B&B Homestay Proprietors Association of Hawaii
1277 Mokulua Dr.
Kailua, HI 96734
808-261-1059

Illinois B&B Association
1191 Franklin
Carlyle, IL 62231
618-594-8313

Indiana B&B Association
350 Indian Boundary Rd.
Chesterton, IN 46304
219-926-5781

Iowa Bed & Breakfast Innkeepers Association
629 1st Ave. E.
Newton, IA 50208
515-792-6833

Kansas B&B Association
1675 W. Patterson Ave.
Ulysses, KS 67880
316-356-2570

B&Bs of Kentucky
Kay Carrol
Rt. 3B Box 20
Springfield, KY 40069
606-336-3075

Louisiana B&B Association
825 Kidder Rd.
Carencro, LA 70520
318-896-6529

Maine Innkeepers Association
305 Commercial St.
Portland, ME 04101-4641
207-773-7670

Maryland B&B Association
P.O. Box 23324
Baltimore, MD 21203
410-886-2452

Minnesota B&B Association
615 W. Hoffman St.
Cannon Falls, MN 55009
517-263-5507

Bed & Breakfast Inns of Missouri
Garth Woodside Mansion
RR 1
Hannibal, MO 63401
314-221-2789

Montana B&B Association
480 Bad Rock Dr.
Columbia, MT 59912
800-453-8870

North Carolina Bed & Breakfast & Inns
318 W. Queen St.
Hillsborough, NC 27278

Nebraska Association of B&B
P.O. Box 2333
Lincoln, NE 68502
402-423-3480

New England Innkeepers Association
P.O. Box 1089
North Hampton, NH 03862
603-964-6689

B&B Innkeepers Association of New Jersey
P.O. Box 164
Stanhope, NJ 07874
609-861-5847

New Mexico B&B Association
P.O. Box 2925
Santa Fe, NM 87504

B&Bs of New York State
P.O. Box 862
Canandaigua, NY 14424
716-394-3569

Ohio Bed & Breakfast Association
3656 Polk Hollow Rd.
Chillicothe, OH 45601
614-774-1770

Oklahoma B&B Association
1841 NW. 15th St.
Oklahoma City, OK 73106
405-521-0011

Oregon B&B Guild
P.O. Box 3187
Ashland, OR 97520
503-482-8707

B&B Division
Pennsylvania Travel Council
c/o Wedgewood Inn
111 W. Bridge St.
New Hope, PA 18938
215-862-2570

Tennessee B&B Innkeepers Association
P.O. Box 5277
Sevierville, TN 37862
615-453-9832

B&B Society of Texas
7114 Eicher Dr.
Houston, TX 77036
713-771-3919

Bed & Breakfast Inns of Utah
P.O. Box 3066
Park City, UT 84060
801-645-8068

B&B Association of Virginia
501 Richmond Rd.
Williamsburg, VA 23185
800-776-0570

Washington B&B Guild
1388 Moore Rd.
Mount Vernon, WA 98273
206-445-6805

Wisconsin B&B Homes & Historic Inns Association
405 Collins St.
Plymouth, WI 53073
414-892-2222

Wyoming Homestay & Outdoor Adventure
Box 579
Big Horn, WY 82833
307-674-8150

Consultants

Almost as quickly as B&Bs have been popping up all over the country, there has been a bevy of consultants to help prospective hosts locate an existing business or start one of their own, and teach them through conventions, seminars or one-on-one meetings. In many cases the people who work as consultants also operate B&Bs of their own, or have in the past, so they have plenty of first-hand experience to draw on and help steer their clients towards the best situation. Some consultants will also hook you up with a B&B where you can intern to see if you're truly cut out for the business.

New seminars and conventions for aspiring and experienced B&B owners are starting up all the time. A reservation service in Newport, Rhode Island, started an annual convention for B&B hosts and innkeepers in New England in 1993, and it proved to be so successful that they held two conventions the next year and started publishing a newsletter. There are similar conventions all over the country. The best way to find one in your area is to check the notices and advertisements in the newsletters published by the national and regional B&B

associations, as well as the independent publications for the trade.

Here's a partial list of consultants who may or may not also serve as convention and seminar organizers.

Oates & Bredfeldt
P.O. Box 1162
Brattleboro, VT 05302
802-254-5931

Ron Kay
Two Suns Limited
1705 Bay St.
Beaufort, SC 29902
803-522-1122

Tom King
Queen Anne B&B
2147 Tremont Pl.
Denver, CO 80205
303-296-6666

Lester & Francoise Roddy
Woods House B&B
333 N. Main St.
Ashland, OR 97520
503-488-1598

Debbie Miller
Bed & Breakfast Enterprises
P.O. Box 3005
Broadway Station
Newport, RI 02840
800-671-7666

Susan Parker
1701 Garnett Creek Ct.
Calistoga, CA 94515
707-942-6905

Courses and Seminars

Many of the convention organizers mentioned previously also hold special workshops for prospective B&B hosts. The best thing to do is to write to the organizers and ask to be placed on their mailing list so you can be alerted to upcoming workshops and seminars. Most last a few days and provide you with a condensed birds-eye view of the business. Some involve strictly sit-down classroom learning, while others emphasize the hectic hands-on method where you hit the ground running by helping out in all departments of a busy B&B. These usually begin Friday and don't let up until the participants collapse Sunday afternoon.

I've also seen B&B courses offered by community colleges and adult schools, so you might want to check your local listings. Even if you aspire to a rural B&B, a workshop in an urban setting will still inform you about many of the ups and downs involved in running a successful B&B.

David Caples
Lodging Resources
P.O. Box 1210
Amelia Island, FL 32034
904-277-4851

Vermont Off Beat
P.O. Box 4366
South Burlington, VT 05406
802-863-2535

Carol Emerick
B&B Resources
P.O. Box 3292
San Diego, CA 92103

Kit Riley
Sage Blossom Consulting
333 Hickok Pl.
Boulder, CO 80301
303-440-4227

Books

Though this book will provide you with everything you need to know to plan and operate your B&B, there is a significant amount of specific information published by the B&B associations and independent organizations to help B&B hosts navigate the stickier subjects of running a B&B. For instance, PAII's *Guide to the Guidebooks* provides a description of most of the travel books published in which B&Bs are featured or frequently reviewed, along with information on how you can contact the author and/or publisher for possible inclusion. (See Chapter 7, for more information on this topic.)

Following is a list of titles that will help B&B hosts run their businesses more effectively.

Available from PAII (805-569-1853):
Guide to the Inn Guidebooks
B&B/Country Inns Industry Survey & Analysis
Sanitation, Food and Health Regulations of Bed-and-Breakfast/Inns

Available from Inn Marketing (815-939-3509):
Country Inns Yellow Pages
Bed & Breakfast Zoning Handbook
Creative Promotions

Magazines and Trade Journals

Again, many of the B&B and tourism associations publish specialized newsletters that address the many topics that concern their members, as well as provide insight into how recently passed legislation and tax information affect the industry. There are independent journals as well.

Here are some of these.

Travel Marketing Bulletin
Williams Hill Publishing
RR 1, Box 1234
Grafton, NH 03240
800-639-1099

Inn Times
2101 Crystal Plaza Arcade
Suite 246
Arlington, VA 22202-4600
202-363-9305

Bed & Breakfast Magazine
4141 N. Scottsdale Rd., Suite 316
Scottsdale, AZ 85251
602-990-1101

Suppliers

It's not too difficult to locate suppliers who will deliver the materials you need to run a B&B. Because you're going to be serving only one meal, with numbers too small to interest a wholesaler, you're probably going to be shopping for food yourself at the supermarket. However, there are many other products and services you can order from companies that specialize in dealing with small business owners and B&B hosts like yourself. Though you certainly don't have to fill your

B&B with every one of the items available, it's a good idea to know what's available in case you want to upgrade at some point in the future.

Following is a list of companies and the products they provide.

Flags and Banners

Gregory Cook
Creative Director
Accent Banner Corporation
2267 Massachusetts Ave.
Cambridge, MA 02140
800-367-3710 or 617-876-1040

Linens

Innstyle
22-28 South Main St.
Doylestown, PA 18901
800-877-4667

Bedding Down
5381 Eagle St.
White Bear Lake, MN 55110
612-429-0921

Eldridge House Corporation
549 Middle Neck Rd.
Great Neck, NY 11023
800-622-0272

Beds and Furniture

The Bedpost
32 S. High St.
East Bangor, PA 18103
610-588-4667

Elizabeth Long Furniture
334 E. Bay St.
Suite G-236
Charleston, SC 29401
803-722-7262

Lawrence Crouse
Whippersnapper Country Furniture
Rt 1, Box 6
Leetown Pike
P.O. Box 606
Kearneysville, WV 25430
304-876-6325

Bathroom Fixtures

Bathroom Machineries
495 Main St.
P.O. Box 1020
Murphys, CA 95247
209-728-2031

Antique Hardware Store
R.D. 2, Box A-IR1
Kintnersville, PA 18930
215-847-2447

Innsitters

Mary Kohler
Time Out For Innkeepers
R.R. 1, Box 66
West St.
North Bennington, VT 05257
802-442-7318

Shannon Davis
The Innkeeper's Relief
P.O. Box 1408
Nevada City, CA 95959
916-477-7815

Gail Reinertson
Innsitter
1551 Live Oak Dr.
Tallahassee, FL 32301
904-878-2643

Postcards

Mitchell Graphics
2363 Mitchell Park Rd.
Petoskey, MI 49770
800-841-6793

Brochures

PRO Studio
1602-C Lake Harbin Rd.
Morrow, GA 30260
404-961-4759

Studio East
P.O. Box 2079
Fort Lee, NJ 07024
201-854-6606

George and Roberta Gardner Photography
Rt 22N
P.O. Box 338
Hillsdale, NY 12529
518-325-3026 or 413-528-9199

Customized Mugs

Peter Deneen
c/o Cloth & Clay, Inc.
2325 Endicott
St. Paul, MN 55114
612-646-0238

Innkeepers Exchange

IBBEX
P.O. Box 615
Hayden, ID 83835
208-772-1994

Organizational Software

Jeff Koss
JK Software Systems
The InnManager
28 Chapel St.
Portsmouth, NH 03801
603-433-3252

Gene McAllister
The Front Desk
Box 1706
Guerneville, CA 95446
707-869-3121

Mulberry Computers
P.O. Box 361943
Milpatis, CA 95036
800-999-1955

Murder Mystery Parties

PostMortem
800-535-PLOT

Guest Registers, Journals, Imprinted Pens

French Creek Press
Box 249
Kimberton, PA 19442
610-983-0774

Metal Graphics
5307 Lee Highway
Arlington, VA 22207-1669
703-237-8223

Note Cards and Stationery
with Pen and Ink Drawing of Your B&B

Don McKillop
Pendragon Creatives
Six Milk St.
Salem, MA 01970
508-741-1362

Deborah Springer
280 Alder Lane
Boulder, CO 80304
303-443-7939

Charles Marton
Artist
P.O. Box 328
Hannawa Falls, NY 13647
315-268-8667

Insurance

James W. Wolf Insurance
P.O. Box 510
Ellicott City, MD 21044
800-488-1135

Arndt McBee Insurance Agency
P.O. Box 1106
Martinsburg, WV 25401
800-825-4667

Vicki Dawson
Potter, Leonard & Cahan
P.O. Box 82840
Kenmore, WA 98028
800-548-8857

Soaps and Toiletries

Carol Huntwork
Greenwich Bay Trading Company
5809 Triangle Dr.
Raleigh, NC 27613
919-781-5008

Essential Amenities
Nine Law Dr.
Fairfield, NJ 07004
201-882-8441 or 800-541-6775

Fullers' Soaps
6 Pamaron Way
Novato, CA 94949
415-883-8881

B&B Real Estate Brokers

B&B Assistance
Colorado Inn Brokers
2151 Tremont Pl.
Denver, CO 80205
303-296-6666

Robert Fuehr
The Inn Broker
P.O. Box 79
Okemos, MI 48805
800-926-INNS

Thomas Franco
Badger Realty
P.O. Box 750, Main St.
North Conway, NH 03860
603-356-5757

Cleaning Supplies

The Clean Team
2264 Market St.
San Francisco, CA 94114
415-621-8444

Universal Hotel Supply Company
4516 S Western Ave.
Los Angeles, CA 90062
213-295-5200

T-Shirts, Jackets, Caps

Sage Advertising and Promotional Products
P.O. Box 1187, 350 Bedford St.
Lakeville, MA 02347
800-321-1045

Quilts

Pinestead Quilts
2059 Easton Rd.
Franconia, NH 03580
603-823-8080

Small Business Administration

The Small Business Administration, which you help to fund with your tax dollars, is a veritable gold mind of information. There are three major divisions within the Small Business Administration that can assist you in the start-up phase of your business, as well as provide you with advice and assistance once your business is up and running.

One is the Small Business Development Center, which counsels entrepreneurs in every conceivable type of business and at every level of development. The SBDC will set you up in private sessions with an entrepreneur who has experience running a B&B, or at least has hands-on experience in the hospitality industry. There, you can ask about any phase of running a B&B, from marketing to locating suitable financing and to keeping the business going in tough times.

The SBA also runs the Small Business Institute (SBI) on a number of college campuses nationwide. Each SBI tends to specialize in a given field, from engineering to business management, but if you're looking for very specific information contact the nearest SBI that has the program you want. The SBI offers consulting services, largely provided by students in the program but always under the watchful eye of a professor or administrator.

The Service Corps of Retired Executives, or SCORE can be an exciting place for you to get information about your business. SCORE officers provide one-on-one counseling with retired business people who volunteer their time to help entrepreneurs get the help they need. Each volunteer counselor has extensive experience in a particular field and is eager to share his insights. SCORE also offers a variety of seminars and workshops on all aspects of business ownership where you'll get specific advice about the nuts and bolts of running a business, from bookkeeping to taxes.

The Small Business Administration also has a program to help small businesses get financing, but you have to apply for a loan through a bank. The SBA then kicks in some of the funds and guarantees your loan to the lender. The SBA also offers a large variety of helpful booklets and brochures on all aspects of running a business.

To locate the SBA and its other programs, look in the white pages of the phone book under United States Government. Call the office nearest you for information about the programs and services they provide locally.

To contact the SBA in Washington directly, write to them at:

The Small Business Administration
409 Third St. S.W.
Washington, DC 20416

To get in touch with the variety of services, call these numbers for immediate help:

SBA Answer Desk 800-827-5722

If you have a computer and modem, you can go online with the SBA at 800-697-4636

Other Small Business Organizations

Once you start your B&B, you'll be joining the millions of other Americans who are owning and operating small businesses. Specific questions can pop up, and you'll undoubtedly want to network with other entrepreneurs who aren't necessarily in the same field.

There are a number of nationwide associations that provide small business owners with information, specific resources, discounts on business products and services, and the ability to work with other members. The government also gets into the act.

Here's a listing of a number of nationwide organizations that have proven to be valuable to the entrepreneurs who join them.

National Association for the Self-Employed
P.O. Box 612067
Dallas, TX 75261
800-232-6273

National Association of Home Based Businesses
10451 Mill Run Circle
Suite 400
Owings Mills, MD 21117
410-363-3698

National Federation of Independent Business
600 Maryland Ave. S.W.
Suite 700
Washington, DC 20024
202-554-9000

American Woman's Economic Development Corporation
71 Vanderbilt Ave.
Suite 320
New York, NY 10169
800-222-2933

National Association of Women Business Owners
1377 K St. N.W.
Suite 637
Washington, DC 20005
301-608-2590

National Minority Business Council
235 E. 42 St.
New York, NY 10017
212-573-2385

Action Guidelines

✔ Use your own experiences to set the tone for your B&B. This is what will make guests happy.

✔ Join a trade association.

✔ Contact some B&B consultants for expert advice, or take a few courses.

✔ Subscribe to some trade journals and newspapers.

✔ Contact suppliers to see how you can increase the attractiveness of your B&B by using their customized products.

✔ Get in touch with the Small Business Administration for specialized business advice.

B&B Profile

Darlene Fain
MeadowHaven B&B
Germanton, North Carolina

"Be ready to make a long-term commitment," says Darlene Fain, who runs MeadowHaven B&B with her husband, Sam, in advising aspiring B&B hosts. "Be prepared for tons of laundry, and have a lot of humility."

Once B&B owners start taking in guests, it's a sure bet that they're going to get bookings a year in advance. So you've got to commit that you'll be around in a year, which is a long time in the B&B business. Fain mentions humility in response to the many misconceptions that new B&B hosts have. "They figure if they have this big house they're just going to be running the B&B, but with 2,000 guests coming in and out of your home over the course of a year, that means 2,000 toilets you'll have to clean." In addition to laundry that never seems to end, this makes for a very long year.

But when it comes right down to it, Darlene and Sam wouldn't have it any other way. They opened MeadowHaven in December 1992 with three guest rooms. The Fains have drawn on their experience in the hospitality industry. Darlene had worked with the Marriott Corporation for five years, and Sam was a chef. They had a chance to build a house in the country in an area where there were no other lodging facilities besides their future B&B. From the time the Fains built their house and decided to open a B&B to when they greeted their first guests, six months elapsed. They had to add several bathrooms, do a lot of landscaping, and get a routine together. Also, they had to decide how they were going to respond to guests and how much attention to give them.

From her experience in the travel industry, Darlene knew that most people want something special when they travel. "And that's what a B&B should provide, since people are willing to pay for it," she says. "When we visited other B&Bs we felt they were inferior to our standards and details. Mostly it was the little things, like cleanliness, having trash can liners and wooden hangers. Also, we occasionally ran into rude hosts, which we haven't figured out yet. Why get into the business if you don't enjoy it?"

And the Fains do enjoy the business, but it is difficult at times. "It really ties you down," she says. "It's like babysitting for adults all the time. Someone always has to be there—I don't know how one person manages to do it all."

In fact, Darlene and Sam enjoy the business so much that they're expanding their B&B by adding a few cabins onto their land , all with fireplaces and hot tubs. "We learn something new every day from our guests, and one of the most surprising was how many people want a whirlpool tub in their rooms. They're willing to pay the difference."

With B&Bs still growing in popularity, many people who have never before stayed at a B&B come to MeadowHaven. Here, Darlene is candid: "Some of these people we wouldn't have back," she says. "They're not people who you'd want to stay in your home, but once they're here we have no choice. They don't know how to behave, and they think they're in a hotel. We tell them the check-in time, but they don't get here until very late. Some insist on smoking even though we have a no-smoking policy. Most things, actually, you don't find out until they leave. And then if they call back to make another reservation, we'll tell them we're booked."

Darlene markets the B&B through write-ups in many of the inn and B&B guidebooks and advertising in local newspapers and the Yellow Pages. MeadowHaven is also listed on a reservation service on Prodigy, an online service, and she sends out a regular newsletter to the 700 previous guests on her mailing list. Many couples stay at MeadowHaven for their honeymoon, and to these couples Darlene promotes a special one-year anniversary discount package called The Lovebird's Retreat.

The B&B gets more pleasure travelers than business people since it is out of the way, not near a town or major city. Rooms range from $60 to $85 a night and include breakfast. Darlene says that the higher priced rooms always go first.

It's been a lot of work opening and the promoting the B&B, but Darlene says that it's definitely been worth it. However, if they were to do it over again, Darlene says that they would have bought an existing B&B. "That way, you get a lot quicker start with the business, and you have immediate income," she says. "It's definitely easier."

Chapter 4

PLANNING

Planning is the key to the success of your B&B. I believe that starting your B&B business—or any business—without adequate planning is like setting out for a cross-country car trip without a map. You'll spend a good deal of time relying on the advice of other people to give you information on where to go and how to get there.

Take the time now to plan your B&B down to the smallest detail. It's the single most important thing you can do for your future success.

Planning to Succeed

Before starting a B&B—or any business for that matter—every entrepreneur *expects* to succeed. However, only a handful *plan* to succeed.

Planning to succeed means you'll have to envision your B&B, and with this vision in mind, write a business plan and a marketing plan. Though many businesses do succeed without developing these plans, it's easier to succeed if you do take the time to plot out every aspect of your business, from the magazines in which you'd like to advertise to the color of the quilts on the beds.

Getting the details in writing months—or even years—before your first guest arrives not only helps to clarify your vision but also provides you with a blueprint so you can check every so often to see that you're on target and on schedule. Take the time now to plan your business. Later on, it may be too late.

Unplanned Failure

Even with the best of intentions and the most detailed business and marketing plans, sometimes a B&B will fail or at least seriously underperform the owner's initial business projections. Perhaps the owners' expectations were overly optimistic and their budget didn't allow for much leeway. And sometimes events beyond their control can occur—like a prolonged downturn in the economy, or a snowless winter for a B&B located near a ski resort—and they won't be able to salvage a business no matter how good the business plan.

The most common reasons of failure in the B&B industry are lack of capital and not enough marketing. Even though most business and marketing plans do account for these factors, most people underestimate the amount of cash they'll need to pay the bills during slow times, and the time they'll need to spend on marketing just to get their names out and keep them there. Another little-mentioned reason why B&Bs fail is that despite everything they read and all the workshops and seminars aspiring B&B hosts attend, most people still vastly underestimate the amount of time and energy running a B&B requires. Couples especially who run the business as a joint venture may be particularly surprised at the wedge the business can drive into their relationship if they're not careful. Vastly different management styles that they weren't aware of way back when they first decided who would prepare breakfast each day may also interfere.

As you take the three major steps to avoiding failure—envisioning your B&B, writing a business plan, and writing a marketing plan—be aware of anything that causes little alarms to go off in your brain—it might be the prospect of keeping only $1,000 in an emergency fund account or someone's suggestion that you can achieve an average of 75 percent occupancy in your first six months of business. You're right to stop, take a deep breath, and go for a walk. Listen to these warning signals and try to put some perspective into what it's like to run a B&B before you start. The best way to avoid failure is if you can regard all income from the B&B as additional income, or else as money to plow back into the business, rather than revenue you have to depend on to pay the mortgage and taxes. Of course, that means you might have to start with only one or two rooms while you or your partner—or both of you—are still working at a full-time job or running another business from home, but many experienced B&B hosts suggest that you start slowly and expand the business only when you can. That way, the mistakes you make will still be manageable, and you won't panic when you need to replace the furnace or fix the roof when you have no guests, because you'll still have income—and savings.

Envisioning Your B&B

Before you get into the nuts and bolts of writing a business and marketing plan for your B&B, now is a perfect time to fantasize about how you see your B&B. What kind of furniture do you want in the guest rooms? How will you landscape the yard? What will you serve for breakfast? You may want to answer these questions twice: once for how you envision your B&B in the beginning, and again for a year or more later, after are able to make the improvements you want. If you're opening your B&B with a partner, both of you should separately fill out this form and compare your answers. If any of your answers are radically different, you should address them now to avoid unnecessary expense and disagreements later.

- What would you like to name your B&B?
- How many rooms?
- What style—formal, country, Victorian, antique, or grandmother's attic?
- What are the common areas that you will make available to guests?
- What kind of breakfast will you serve: continental with pastries, fruit and coffee, or a full hot meal, with eggs, pancakes, meat, and toast?
- Do the rooms have private or shared baths? Will you convert any?
- What extra touches will be in the rooms? List them.
- What kinds of books will you place in the rooms?
- What times of day do you see yourself visiting with guests?
- What kind of sign will you hang out front?
- Who will do the cooking? Who will clean?
- What will be on your answering machine announcement tape? Or will you hire an answering service?
- What other touches do you want to add that will make your B&B the kind of place you'd like to visit?
- What's important to you when you stay in a B&B? Try to incorporate these factors into your own vision.

Writing Your Business Plan

Why should you write a business plan? You have a good idea of what you want to do—open a B&B—where it will be located, and when you want to do it. Even if your goals are not that specific at this point, you probably have an idea of the type of B&B you'd like to run.

Writing a business plan will help you to map out a specific blueprint for meeting your goals. A business plan allows no question about the smallest aspect of starting your B&B; without it many things will get overlooked in the confusion and excitement. Getting all the details in writing provides you with a detailed itinerary. And since you write the plan yourself, you'll tailor it to your own needs and also to tinker with it later when unforeseen roadblocks begin to emerge.

With a business plan in hand, you'll be able to show the banker, your suppliers, and other potential business contacts exactly how you envision your B&B, in language and figures they understand. Also, the act of writing will reveal a lot of thought and ideas that might not have come up otherwise.

Writing a business plan before you do anything else for your B&B will put you way ahead of your competition, since most businesses do not take the time beforehand to plan out their strategies so carefully.

Although a business plan is an important step to the successful start-up of a B&B, it is meant to be used and referred to as you go. Periodically checking the progress you're making against the goals you put forth in the plan allows you to see where changes need to be made. Spend the time now on your business plan—if you run into trouble later on and don't have a business plan to refer back to, it just might be too late.

Anyone who reads your business plan will be able to get a clear picture of the type of B&B you'd like to run, as well as its projected financial health.

A business plan can be a few pages long, or a massive 100-page document that maps out every single detail involved in running your B&B. Though it takes more time, it's best to err on the side of quantity when writing a business plan for your B&B. The more you know about your business before you take in your first guest, the better prepared you will be for the surprises that will inevitably happen.

Figure 4.1 (p. 74) is an outline of the format of a business plan. Refer to Appendix A for the complete plan.

Figure 4.1

Business Plan Outline

- Cover Sheet—List name of business and all principals along with an address and phone number.

- Statement of Purpose—Briefly state your objectives.

- Table of Contents

- Section One: The Business—Describe the business. What will you provide the customers? Who are your target markets? Where will you be located? Who is your competition? What personnel do you expect to hire?

- Section Two: The Finances—Include income projections and cash flow projections. If you're buying an existing business, include its financial history under the previous owner.

- Section Three: Supporting Documents—Back up the information in the previous sections. Include a résumé of your previous employment history, your credit report, and letters of reference along with any other items you believe will help the reader better grasp how you plan to operate your business.

Writing Your Marketing Plan

Though you do cover marketing to some extent in your business plan, developing and writing a separate, detailed marketing plan will serve the same clarifying purpose to your marketing efforts as the business plan does for the development and daily operations of your B&B.

You do have a lot of ideas to choose from in Chapter 7, but without a concrete plan to follow it's easy to let marketing fall to the bottom of your daily and weekly to-do lists, or even fall off entirely.

As in a business plan, in your marketing plan you'll define your purpose and target market as well as the various tools in your marketing arsenal. You'll design a marketing budget that is reasonable and aggressive at the same time, pick your media and describe the methods you'll use to evaluate results. This review will help you to adjust your marketing plan for the following year.

For small businesses that can't afford to hire a full-time marketing specialist, anything that involves promotional activity of any kind usually invites a shrug—or a sneer. After all, marketing is not most people's idea of a good time.

Marketing is often an afterthought, a task that is performed grudgingly when an advertising deadline looms or after you attend a trade association meeting and decide that your brochure and other promotional materials look painfully out-of-date compared to everyone else's.

One way to make marketing your business tolerable and even sometimes enjoyable is to map out a specific plan each year that won't let you off the hook so easily. If you say that in March you'll send out your new brochure and guest newsletter, and budget for it, you'll probably do it.

The primary mistake that small businesses make in their marketing is to rely too heavily on advertising. I'm not saying that advertising doesn't work, because in some cases it can pull quite well. However, it often turns out to be the most expensive and least effective way to reach customers, especially when your one-inch display ad is only one of hundreds.

Advertising is a known entity with a tangible product—but it doesn't necessarily produce the results you desire, which is an increase in the number of customers. Advertising is easy because you tell the sales rep what you want to say, you write out a check, go over the proof, and receive a copy of the magazine. In other words, somebody else does all the work. Spending your time and money on promotion—whether it's sending out a press kit or hosting a travel writer—is harder, and doesn't provide you with a guaranteed output (i.e., an ad in print), but what it will do is provide you with increased exposure among your targeted customers. They'll notice you simply because you'll stand out. After all, the majority of businesses take the easy way out, spending the bulk of their annual marketing budget on advertising and perhaps printing another 1,000 copies of their brochure with what's left over. In planning your marketing, consider each of the following programs and how you can combine them to get your message across.

Advertising—Radio, newspaper, TV, magazines, and directories of various trade associations.

Direct Mail—Sending brochures to prospective and past customers, writing and editing a newsletter, or sending information to businesses that might book rooms for visiting business people, or renting your business for a special function.

Publicity—Sending letters, press releases, and kits; making follow-up calls; and offering a complimentary visit to members of the press in exchange for the possibility of a writeup. This can consist of a full feature or a mention of your company in a roundup, or service piece.

Special Events—Planning special events, working with the chamber of commerce and other travel businesses.

Developing a plan will help you to take a long-range view to spread your efforts among a variety of marketing opportunities. It will also help you to anticipate certain events that only happen once a year. But the plan is also meant to be tinkered with. For example, if a specific advertising issue comes up in September, or you hear about an idea that has worked wonders for another similar business nearby and you want to try it, you may look at November and December and see you don't have much scheduled even though your monthly marketing budget allows for $100. So you take the money from those two months and are able to pay for the project.

There are a number of different aspects to a marketing plan. The type of customer you'd like to attract also enters into each of these aspects, broken down by region, profession, sex, income, and interests.

1. The amount of time you will spend marketing, on both a daily and weekly basis.

2. The type of marketing you plan to do, from concentrating on magazine publicity or newspaper ads to revamping your brochure and business cards.

3. The amount of money you want to budget for each month and for the total year.

Who's going to carry out each task? For some businesses, only one person will be responsible for writing copy, working with a graphic artist, and doing interviews with the press. Even in the smallest businesses, some business owners decide to spread out the responsibilities to insure they get done and to provide a fresh eye.

To draw up your annual marketing plan, you'll have to answer a lot of questions. You'll need to be as complete as possible, however, to design the best marketing plan for your business. The questions shown in Figure 4.2 on p. 78 make a good starting point.

Refer to Appendix B for an example of what a typical annual marketing plan looks like. The business is for a five-room country inn located in a tourist area in northern New England.

Starting Your B&B from Scratch

If you decide to start your B&B from scratch, whether you use the house you're currently living in or need to buy a house to accommodate the business, you will need to do more work

Figure 4.2:

Market Planning Assessment

TIME

How much time do you spend each week on marketing?

Provide a breakdown of how many hours you'll spend each week on publicity, advertising, direct mail, and other areas. Do you feel this is enough time? Do you think you're using your time effectively?

Would you like to spend more or less time? What would you spend it on, or where would you cut back?

When are your busiest seasons? How far in advance should you begin planning for the various media and projects that you want to do?

Look back over the last calendar year. Which months were slow in terms of business? Which were busy?

MEDIA

In which media would you like to focus more of your marketing efforts?

What type of marketing brings you the most customers?

BUDGET

What percentage of total sales does your marketing budget comprise? How could you increase—or decrease—that amount? What other categories could you take money from?

Do you have an annual or a monthly marketing budget now?

Would you like to invest more money in one or more categories? Which ones? Why?

EXECUTION

Name the person or people currently responsible for marketing. Is there anyone else you feel comfortable assigning additional duties?

Are there additional tasks you could assign to a staff member that you don't like to do or don't have enough time for?

CUSTOMERS

In which area of the country do most of your customers live? Are they urban professional types?

What type of customer would you like to see more of? How can you target them? Why would they be attracted to your business?

Think about your answers to these questions for a few days. Is there anything missing?

than if you bought an existing B&B. The advantage is that it costs less; the downside is that it will take more time before you open your B&B, unless you will use your current house and do the planning in your spare time.

There's also a lot more detail and legal work to do if you start from scratch, including getting a business license, passing a health and fire inspection, and setting yourself up as a business, all of which is covered in Chapter 5.

The main disadvantage to starting a B&B from scratch is that you won't have income from the business until you open the B&B, which usually always takes longer than your initial estimates. In fact, while you do pay more at the outset for an existing B&B, the business can start producing revenue for you from the day you move in. In fact, several B&B owners who started from scratch say that if they had to do it all over again, they would buy an existing B&B. You should weigh the pros and cons against your own temperament before you proceed.

If you buy an existing B&B, most of it has already been set up for you, from the lodging to the license to the insurance—though you do have to change everything over into your name.

Buying a B&B

Though you still need to write business and marketing plans, you have the advantage of a track record to which you can compare your own efforts. However, there are dangers to buying a B&B that you should be aware of. Since a B&B is such a personalized experience for most guests, be prepared for the following exchange after you assume ownership.

"Good afternoon, Mountain Crest Bed & Breakfast. Can I help you?"

"Oh, who's this?"

"Jean Carver. I own the B&B."

"Where's Bob Loomis (the previous owner)?"

"He moved to Florida, and I bought the B&B from him a couple of months ago."

"Oh, is he running a B&B down there?"

"No, he retired."

"Oh, well. Good-bye then."

There are guests who feel such a loyal connection with certain B&B hosts that they feel that if they reserve a room with you it wouldn't be the same, and would be a betrayal of the previous owners. The majority of guests, however, won't be so single-minded and will give you a chance—if they need to stay at a place in the area and aren't just coming to visit the owner.

Buying a B&B means that you have the advantage of a hopefully good reputation, and an established list of customers who are familiar with your B&B. In addition, frequent visitors to your area may already know about the B&B even if they haven't stayed there in the past, which provides another pool of potential customers for you to pursue.

Sometimes, buying an existing B&B will actually cost less than starting from scratch if you factor in all of the furniture, equipment, and other amenities that are included in the purchase price. And if you figure that your labor is worth something, even though you probably won't be paying yourself a salary for quite some time, buying a B&B outright may turn out to be a veritable bargain.

Evaluating an Opportunity

If you're starting from scratch, you'll have less to evaluate than if you plan to buy a B&B. The first—and by far most important—thing to consider is your location. If you're situated in an area where a significant number of transients pass through your town, your marketing efforts will focus on your B&B, and not how to attract people to the area in the first place. Barring that, it helps if you're located near a college or private school, or major business district. In this case, your marketing efforts will consist of contacting the individuals who field calls from parents of students who need a place to stay, or business people who host other business people from out of the area.

If you're buying a B&B, of course you should also consider the issue of location, but you'll need to comb the books, ask neighbors about the B&B—if the neighbors are enemies, they can create very large problems for you and your guests—and also call previous guests for their impressions.

Even after all this, however, deciding whether or not to start or buy a B&B comes down to your own initial gut reaction: If it feels right, then go ahead and do it. After all, the B&B will also serve as your home as well as your business, and your guest's home away from home. If you don't feel good about it, your guests won't either.

Action Guidelines

✔ Plan to start slowly when you open your B&B, and build gradually from there.

✔ Describe your B&B down to the smallest detail.

✔ Write your business plan for your B&B.

✔ Write your B&B marketing plan.

✔ Determine whether buying an existing B&B or starting from scratch would make the most sense for you.

Chapter
5

STARTING UP

lanning and executing all the factors and details involved
in starting a business usually serves as the testing ground
of a business: After all, if you're still enthusiastic about
running a B&B after you've gotten through all this grunt work
then you know you've made the right decision.

Even if you've fallen out of love with your B&B after the
start-up tasks, you shouldn't worry, because the moment your
first guest walks through the door all the reasons for entering
the business in the first place will come rushing back at you.

You just have to jump through a few hoops first.

How to Test Your Business Idea

The best way to see if your area can support a B&B, whether
a new or existing business, is to talk with the owners of the
other lodging businesses in town and with tourism people
who frequently book rooms for travelers.

First talk to other B&B hosts in the area. Some may not
want to talk with you, since they may view you as potential
competition, but surprisingly enough, most of the people who
are in the hospitality business regard other lodging facilities as
cooperators, not competitors. After all, when they're booked

up and need to refer a guest to another place in town to stay, they may call you with the expectation that you'll reciprocate in the future when you're in the same situation. In fact, one of the major reasons why many B&Bs form associations is so they can promote themselves as a group more effectively.

When you speak with lodging owners, find out about the busy and slow times of the year in the area. Where do their guests come from and how do the B&Bs market to them? Is there another business or tourist attraction in town that frequently steers guests to the B&B? If you're starting from scratch, ask owners if they feel the need for another B&B in town. If you're buying a B&B, ask about the current owners and the reputation that the B&B has with locals as well as with guests. This information can be very revealing. It's a good idea to talk with several people for different perspectives.

You should also talk to the local chamber of commerce as well as the regional and state tourism boards. The state board may give a different perspective than the local chamber, since they have a broader perspective of tourism in the state; they can compare tourism in your area to other parts of the state and provide figures to indicate if tourism is on the rise in your area.

Frequently, these boards hold meetings and seminars for travel business owners on how to increase their business and run their operations more effectively, so it pays to talk with tourism boards in advance and to join them after you start your own B&B.

Selecting Your Business Name

The name of a B&B influences a customer's decision whether or not to book a room there. The names of many B&Bs can be so vague as to not describe the establishment at all. On the other hand, there are some B&Bs where you want to ask the owners why they chose their name.

I haven't heard people say that they chose not to book a room at a B&B because they didn't like the name, but since the name should convey the feel of a B&B, you should take some care when selecting it. Some take the easy route and name the B&B after themselves: Shaw's Inn, The Bailey House, Smith's B&B. Others name their B&B after a specific geographic location: Hilltop Acres B&B, Lakeside House, Black Mountain B&B, or the Inn at Blush Hill. Even though these names are somewhat vague, a prospective guest can still get a feel for what it would be like to stay there. Others name their B&Bs after the year the house was built: The 1897 House or 1902 Victorian B&B.

Then there are those names that are just plain silly, and guests have no idea what to expect. These include names with lots of hyphens and parts of the owners' names arranged to form a made-up word. I also frown on B&Bs with exclamation points in their names or that explain too much: What A View! is one, while The Urban Retreat and Here's R&R don't strike me as places where I'd particularly want to stay. If the names seem somewhat amateurish, I figure that the B&B will follow suit.

Pick three or four different names, then try them out on friends who are honest with you as well as the people at the local chamber of commerce. All this assumes that you're starting a B&B from scratch. If you're buying a B&B, my advice is to stick with its current name. Change it only after a few years when you've established yourself. However, by that time, you probably won't want to.

Registering Your Business

There are always certain legal requirements you must meet before operating any business. Since a B&B involves people staying overnight in your house and eating food prepared in your kitchen, the restrictions are a bit more complex than other businesses that sell strictly a service or retail item.

The first thing you need to do is register your business with the state. There will be a fee for this, and the purpose is to make sure no other business is currently operating with your name. If there is, you will have to find another name for your B&B. Registration will also alert the state to expect tax revenue from your business. If you don't file a return with the state, they'll know where to find you.

Licenses and Permits

When you register with the state, you should also ask about other regulations you have to meet in order to operate as a B&B in your state. Before you spend one penny on renovations or send out an application to be listed in a guidebook, check with the local, county and state business authorities to find out about the various kinds of licenses and permits you'll need and the fire, building, and health codes you'll need to meet. If you neglect any one of the necessary steps to opening and operating a B&B in your town, the government authorities at any level have the power necessary to shut down your business or do whatever is necessary to bring your business up to code. The time to find out all the requirements is before you open your doors. This is important even if you're buying an existing B&B, because the codes may have changed, subject to a grandfather clause, since the owners started their business; the exemptions of such a clause may expire when a new owner assumes the business. Or perhaps, the town fathers have just looked the other way because the owners were friends or family; but they're going to come down hard on you, especially if you're a newcomer to town. If they catch you later, you won't be able to use your ignorance as an excuse. So it pays to do your homework first.

The best thing to do is to ask other B&B owners about all the necessary regulations in addition to checking with the town and state. Either may overlook something, so it's also a good idea to check with the state's B&B association; call the state tourism department for the contact name and number.

These vary from town to town and from state to state, so I'm not going to go into detail about them here.

I will describe only the general purpose of the licenses and permits that will be required. Bear in mind, however, the stringency of these requirements will also vary as well. States and regions with more highly regulated governments tend to be pickier about the quality of your B&B, and the fees they charge you for the privilege of accepting a few guests into your home definitely reflects this.

Even though you may resent all the legalese and paper-work, it's important to meet all of the requirements. No one says you can't complain every step of the way, however. Below is a rundown of the basic requirements.

- In addition to business registration, some states will require you to have a license to operate as a B&B if you have a certain number of rooms or full occupancy above a certain number.

- You'll need a sales tax or lodging tax certificate from the state to collect tax.

- You'll probably need to have the local fire inspector check your home for properly marked fire exits, smoke alarms in each room and adequate construction and protection against fire. In some cases, an older building will pass fire code, but if you plan to renovate or build an entirely new building, the code is more stringent and may include the construction of special firewalls designed to restrict the spread of fire as well as custom fire escapes that can be accessed from each room. Hard-wired smoke and fire detectors are a must in most new construction or renovations, as well. Some fire codes may even require expensive sprinkler systems to be built, along with a fire alarm system.

- A health inspector will ascertain whether your septic and water systems can accommodate the increased demands that regular guests will place on them.

- Some states require that you obtain a restaurant license if you plan to serve meals to outside guests in addition to overnight guests. Others will prohibit a B&B from serving a hot breakfast, depending upon the number of guest rooms, and dictate that pastry be served in cellophane. Most B&B hosts can find a way around this, in the interest of B&B guests, who expect a hot, hearty cooked breakfast, not a stale piece of Danish.

- Even if your home and facilities successfully meet all of the above regulations, if your home is not in an area that is zoned for B&B use, you may be out of luck. Your town government determines zoning and is also responsible for making exceptions for B&Bs and other businesses that are located outside of commercial zones. Though your B&B will provide a tax base for your town and help promote tourism and commerce, if it is a commercial enterprise operating in a residential area, you will probably have to apply for a zoning variance. The rules get creative, though. Some towns will allow you to operate as a B&B in a residential area as long as you don't put a sign out. Others will require that you as owner live in the house and not in a separate building. You may also have to expand your driveway and parking area to accommodate an increased number of cars.

Far more interesting laws governing B&Bs undoubtedly exist. That's why it's important to check all of the requirements *before* you do anything.

Choosing a Legal Structure

While talking with other B&B owners, it's also a good idea to ask about their legal structure: a sole proprietorship, partnership, or a corporation. Each has its advantages and disadvantages, and B&B owners have very specific reasons for picking one over the others.

Sole Proprietorship

A sole proprietorship is the form of business that most single-owner businesses pick. It's easy to start—all you have to do is register with the state and you're in business; you make all the decisions yourself; and aside from zoning and other regulations connected with running a B&B, you're pretty much free from having to follow complex laws regarding the operation of your business. You alone are responsible for the success or failure of your business, and any profits the B&B earns are reported as income in your name.

However, because there are few restrictions on a sole proprietorship when you run into legal or financial trouble, it falls on your shoulders. For instance, a guest who slips and falls on the front steps of your B&B can sue you personally; any savings or investments you have—including your equity in the business itself—is fair game for the guest and a hungry lawyer who sees your beautiful house as a piggy bank that needs to be shaken.

For many B&Bs, liability insurance that's tied in withtheir business or homeowners policy will often be enough to handle a "reasonable" lawsuit and settlement. The remote chances of being hit with a lawsuit and the relative ease of operating this form of business ownership make a sole proprietorship the preferred method of business organization for most B&B owners.

However, if your business should fail, you will be responsible for all outstanding debts incurred during the course of doing business. Failure to pay debts or declaring bankruptcy will be reflected on your personal credit record.

Partnerships

A partnership is essentially two sole proprietorships combined. This means that while the strengths are doubled, so are the inherent weaknesses.

A B&B owner will frequently decide to create a partnership and enter the business with a friend or business colleague.

Married couples sometimes decide to form a partnership for their B&B. Though a partnership means more energy and money for the business than a sole proprietorship, it should be entered into with extreme caution. The best partnerships work when the partners have complementary talents and one leaves the other to do what he or she does best. For instance, one partner may have a background in marketing and day-to-day business operations, while the other loves to cook, clean and care for the appearance of the B&B. As long as each trusts the other to concentrate on their department and interferes only when problems arise, then the partnership will probably do well.

Partnerships usually run into trouble when the partners have similar skills or different ideas about the right way to run a business. For example, when both partners want to cook, decorate the B&B, and mingle with guests and neither wants to deal with bookkeeping, reservations, or staff, there are going to be problems right from the start.

As in a sole proprietorship, if a guest decides to sue, both partners are personally liable. And if the business fails leaving outstanding debts, again, you are both responsible. You should also be aware that if one partner disappears after the failure of a B&B, the other must pay all debts. Be aware of this, because it does happen from time to time.

Corporations

A corporation is best defined as an inanimate object, a business organization with its own needs aside from those of the business itself and subject to financial and legal restrictions. It's more difficult, expensive and time-consuming to form and operate your B&B as a corporation, but it also absolves your formal, personal responsibility in case business sours or a customer or supplier decides to sue.

Another advantage that corporations have over partnerships or sole proprietorships is that they can raise money by selling shares in the business; the only recourse the other two forms have is to borrow money from a bank or from friends.

But a corporation is by nature more unwieldy than the other two because of its responsibility to its shareholders, who are really part-owners. The IRS taxes corporations on a different scale from sole proprietorships and partnerships, and there are even more rules and regulations a corporation must follow on both the state and federal level. Except in the case of a Sub-Chapter S corporation, corporate income is taxed twice—first as income to the corporation, then as dividends to individual shareholders. There are also certain restrictions on the types of operations a corporation can run—some expansion and growth issues, for example, require the approval of stockholders before a project can proceed.

Some B&B owners automatically opt for incorporation to protect personal assets, but the kind of B&B that will benefit most from incorporation is when there are more than two owners. Issues of ownership and decision-making become more complex with three or more owners, so it's easier to rely on a board of directors and group of stockholders, especially since they've invested their money and trust in the business.

Do You Need an Attorney?

Whether or not you choose to use the services of an attorney to help you start your B&B depends on how you view the legal profession and how detail-oriented you are. Some B&B owners swear by their lawyers and consult with them about every decision that needs to be made. Others swear *at* them, and will never use an attorney for anything in their business or personal lives if they can possibly avoid it.

The happy medium is somewhere in between. If you're planning to incorporate your B&B, you'll probably need to use a lawyer. Although more people are learning how to incorporate themselves, the vast majority use a lawyer to help facilitate the process.

If you're buying a B&B or another house for your B&B, you will undoubtedly have to hire an attorney to do a title search and to help prepare a warranty deed for the property. But aside from these tasks, you will probably be able to do most of the tasks involved in starting your B&B without a lawyer.

Do You Need an Accountant?

If you're unsure about the type of business organization that suits you best—sole proprietorship, partnership, or corporation—it's a good idea to consult with an accountant to help you decide. An accountant will analyze your current financial situation, help you determine what you want to gain from the B&B—equity or income—and advise you about how to best achieve your goals.

An accountant can also analyze the books and financial records of a B&B you're considering purchasing. It's a good idea to find an accountant who has some experience working with hospitality and lodging businesses; ask other B&Bs in the area for the names of their accountants. Then call several accountants and interview them to make your choice.

An accountant can also help you set up a realistic budget and a schedule of projected revenues. And if this is the first time you've run a business these professional services can familiarize you with different accounting methods and the tax rates based on projected revenue and the tax codes of your state. An accountant can also recommend methods of bookkeeping that will make the job that much easier when tax season rolls around.

Insurance and Bonds

Before the B&B industry exploded in popularity during the '80s, most B&Bs relied on their standard homeowners' policy to cover themselves in case part of their house was damaged. Unless you had more than a couple of rooms, insurance companies generally looked the other way. The alternative was using commercial insurance agencies accustomed to covering multi-unit hotels and motels and other tourist attractions.

Today, it's a different story. With more than 20,000 B&Bs throughout the country, insuring them with adequate coverage has become big business. A variety of insurance companies that specialize in B&Bs have sprung up throughout the country and want your business.

You should first check with your own insurance agency to see if they have provisions for extra coverage for your guests. If all they have is a commercial lodging policy that offers more coverage than you actually need, shop around for another agency that will fill your needs without overinsuring you. You may also need to update your current homeowners' policy, because some companies prohibit their clients from operating any kind of venture on the insured premises. The insurance company may decide to write a policy similar to that which a landlord would have on a property to cover damage from tenants. Be prepared for the shock of paying two to five times the premium that you're paying now. The theory is that no one will be as careful with your house as you will, and since B&B guests are even more transient than tenants, don't be shocked at the quotes you'll receive from insurance companies.

After homeowner's insurance, liability insurance is the most important policy to carry. You might also want to investigate protection against the theft of guests' property and personal liability, which protects you in case a guest is injured while on your premises.

If you can arrange for one insurance company to cover all of these different kinds of insurance for you, you'll probably save money. The premium you'll pay will also be affected by the deductible and coverage you choose and can vary from a few hundred dollars up to ten thousand or more.

Action Guidelines

✔ Research the local market to determine the need for your B&B.

✔ Pick a name for your B&B.

✔ Find out about the legal requirements from licenses and permits to zoning laws and exemptions.

✔ Determine what form of business you'd like—sole proprietorship, partnership, or corporation.

✔ Contact your insurance agency—or an agency that specializes in B&Bs—about any additional coverage you may need.

B&B Profile

Kathy Reccia
The Book and Blanket Bed and Breakfast
Jay, New York

Many times, travelers who favor B&Bs also favor books. Just direct them to a living room with a few overstuffed chairs and shelves filled with books and you can forget about them for a few hours.

When Kathy Reccia first thought about opening up a B&B, she decided to cut right to the quick and offer accommodations to guests with absolutely no pretenses about the main attractions: books. She even highlights the theme by naming the rooms after Jane Austen, Jack London, and F. Scott Fitzgerald.

Kathy, who runs the B&B with her husband Fred Balzac—another fitting name—was living in Cornwall, New York, downstate from Jay, and working as a copywriter in the direct mail division of Barnes & Noble. Kathy and Fred had been considering the idea of starting a B&B, but they felt that this would come later in life.

And then a number of changes in Fred's career altered their perspective. On several visits to the Adirondack Mountains in upstate New York, they stayed in a few B&Bs while looking for houses they could convert for their B&B business. After a few months, they found a house that would make a perfect B&B. They bought it and proceeded to wait a long 18 months until their house in Cornwall sold and they could start the B&B. Kathy and Fred were still both working full-time, and on weekends Kathy made the trip—almost five hours one way—to stay at the house and fix it up.

While she was working on the house she researched the necessary laws and regulations she'd have to meet for her B&B, and to her pleasant surprise, she found out in her area the answer was "not much." As long as her capacity remained at nine people or less, all she had to do was arrange to pay the rooms and meals tax to the state.

Even before Kathy opened in June of 1993, she started to promote the B&B. First, she paid for a notice in *The Annual Directory of American and Canadian Bed & Breakfasts*, which cost $30 and provided her with a free book to boot. "Even though we weren't quite ready, we did it because they work ahead of time. We've gotten quite a few calls from that," she says.

She also joined the Lake Placid Visitors Bureau, which has a reservation referral service, and the B&B Association of New York, whose annual conference she also attended. Kathy has placed ads in several area magazines where readers circle a pre-assigned number on a postcard and send it into the magazine, which then forwards the names to the advertisers, but she found that it hasn't resulted in any new business.

She was very pleased with the B&B business her first winter, and in March, which is a traditionally slow month, the B&B was fully booked every weekend.

She says that when she was staying at other inns, she asked her hosts for advice on starting a B&B, but she relied on her own instincts when it came to deciding what the theme of her own B&B should be. "I was constantly thinking about what I wanted it to be like, and what was missing, like tissues in the rooms and other details," she says. When she started her B&B, she continued her research by asking her guests if she could get them anything else.

She keeps asking, they keep telling her, and she continues to fine-tune the B&B according to their needs.

OPERATIONS

Operations—the day-to-day routine you set up and follow in order to maintain some semblance of organization in your B&B—is not the most fun or creative part of your business, like visiting with guests or conducting interviews with the press. In fact, operations can be downright boring.

But neglecting these steps and running your daily operations in a haphazard way is the quickest way to drive your B&B into the ground. Take some time now to set daily operations policy; later on, it will mean that you'll have more time for the fun stuff.

Estimating Operating Costs

Every business has cycles when business is booming and when it stops dead in its tracks.

But the lodging and hospitality business—especially a small B&B located in an area that relies heavily on tourism—is notorious for ups and downs that can swing radically several times a year. The bad news is that some expenses—like the mortgage and utilities—remain constant. That's why in many B&B association newsletters and guides, you'll see a great emphasis on promoting off-season business—for the B&Bs that decide to remain open during the down times, that is.

If you are purchasing an existing B&B, estimating your operating costs will be easy. Just ask the current owners for a full year's breakdown of expenses along with the current income statement. If possible, go through the expenses with the owners, asking about the budgeted amounts and the actual expenses. If you are starting from scratch, estimating costs will be a little more difficult. You may want to ask another local B&B owner with a similar style of house—e.g., an old, drafty Victorian with an ancient oil furnace—about her expenses, that is, if she'll give them to you. Barring that, the best way to estimate your operating costs is to contact the suppliers you'll be using. They will probably be very helpful.

Figure 6.1 (pp. 100-101) is a chart that contains all possible expenses you may encounter in running a B&B. I won't provide estimates, since they can vary so widely depending on how many rooms you have, the area of the country, and the condition of your house. It's also a good idea to chart the expenses for each month for a year—some are optional, and you can cut down on some expenses by doing things yourself.

Keeping Good Records

It's important to keep track of your expenses and revenue sources. On the one hand, it will make things easier for you at tax time, but it's also enlightening to know how much you spent on a laundry service last year and to figure out how much money you could save at the end of the year by doing it yourself instead.

There are as many ways to keep records as there are B&B hosts. Some rely on one of several computer programs specially designed for B&B owners, while others stuff receipts in shoe boxes then dump them out and add it all up at the end of the year.

No matter what record-keeping method you choose, make it easy and organize the process so you can update records immediately instead of saving up the work to be done in one lump at the end of the week, monthly, or even yearly. If you're like most B&B owners, you won't be able to find a block of time anywhere in your week unless it's in the middle of the night.

Keeping good records will also help facilitate figuring your tax deductions. And in the unlikely case of a tax audit somewhere down the road, it will help your case if you can show the auditor receipts that provide answers to all questions.

Good records will track your monthly and annual occupancy rate as well as where each guest heard about you. When planning future marketing campaigns, you'll know which ad or promotion brought in the most guests.

Keeping adequate records just makes good common sense. At the very least, get a ledger book. Some business checking accounts now offer a built-in ledger that allows you to break down the checks you write into different expense categories, eliminating the need for a separate ledger.

Pricing Your Rooms

Pricing is always a sticky situation. Some people find it extremely difficult to ask other people for money, and as a result, either undercharge or overcharge. Both scenarios will keep guests away.

The best way to determine what to charge for your rooms is to survey what other B&Bs and inns in your area are charging. The feel of a place has a lot to do with it. If the B&B is a business that gets the special attention of the hosts and is not just one of several vocations to keep the owner afloat financially, the prices will reflect this. As you'd expect, a room with a shared bath costs less. High season and a location in a popular and well-traveled area will also drive the prices higher, as well as having fresh flowers in each guest room. But the biggest draw is a whirlpool bathtub. B&B hosts frequently report that the room with the whirlpool always gets booked first.

The House

Mortgage   _____

Taxes   _____

Insurance   _____

Utilities   _____

Heat   _____

Repairs (anticipated)   _____

Office Expenses

Telephone   _____

Separate fax line   _____

Credit card commissions   _____

Postage   _____

Stationery supplies   _____

Printing   _____

Advertising   _____

Travel agency commissions   _____

Trade association dues and memberships   _____

Accountant and attorney fees   _____

Contract employees, freelancers,
   or consultant expenses   _____

Company Vehicle

Loan   _____

Registration   _____

Figure 6.1: A chart for tracking all the possible expenses you may encounter in running a B&B.

Insurance   _____

Gas   _____

Employee Expenses

Payroll   _____

Taxes   _____

Insurance   _____

Workers' compensation   _____

Bonuses   _____

Discounts   _____

Guest Services

Breakfast food   _____

Toiletries   _____

Laundry and linen service   _____

Bathroom supplies   _____

Special amenities   _____

Capital Improvements

Furniture upgrades   _____

New breakfast dishes and utensils   _____

Sheets, linens and towels   _____

In fact, they also say that the most expensive rooms always go first. The smaller, cheaper rooms can actually sometimes be a tough sell.

Bear in mind these are just averages, but I've seen rooms in a family-oriented B&B in rural New England with decorations and furniture that haven't been revamped for guests' tastes priced from $35 to $60 a night, double occupancy. Rooms in fancier, more elegant B&Bs with antique furniture and private baths and where the owners live in a separate dwelling start around $75 and can go up to $150 double occupancy a night. Single occupancy is sometimes charged at a 50 percent discount plus anywhere from $5 to $20 as a single supplement.

Sometimes guests will ask for an extra cot or bed in a room. Most B&Bs that offer this service charge $10 for an extra person and bring in a rollaway bed or have a pullout couch already in the room. Similarly, many B&Bs charge $10 for any child who stays in the room with the parents, if children are welcome at the B&B. I've also seen some B&Bs that charge the same amount to accommodate a dog.

Discounts for multiple night stays—from three or four nights up to a week or more—usually earn a 10 percent or more discount. However, these discounts are usually promoted as a special offer, as in if you stay two nights, you'll get one free. Since the majority of guests will book three nights in a row at the most, and be perfectly willing to pay for it, there's no need to offer the discount except in the off-season, when any reservations are welcome.

Accounting Basics

In running your B&B, you need to keep track of revenue coming in and expenses going out. It's a good idea to set up an accounting system appropriate for you and your business.

There are two kinds of accounting you can use to track revenue and expenses. One, *cash accounting,* involves simple bookkeeping where income is recorded when it is received, and expenses are recorded when they are paid, even if the expense was incurred in a different month. For instance, say a guest spends three nights with you on the last few days of a month. You deposit her check or charge her room rate and other expenses to her credit card, but the income is not posted in your account until a few days later, which happens to fall in the next month. With cash accounting, you will record the revenue in the month in which the funds were posted to your accounts, which may give you an inaccurate picture of your business cycles if you rely on revenue alone to show the health of your business, and not month-to-month occupancy rate. Cash accounting, however, is a very simple way to keep your books, and B&B owners for whom the business is one of several income-generating vocations, prefer it for its simplicity. They don't need a precise picture of their month to month revenue and expense picture.

Accrual accounting is more painstaking in its execution but gives a more accurate view of revenue and expenses and of your monthly financial situation. Even though payment may be received or credited the following month and expenses paid on a net 30 system, they are recorded in the current month's ledgers, when incurred, rather than actually paid.

When drawing up your accounting sheets, no matter which method you choose, refer to the categories named in the previous section, Estimating Operating Costs. You may want to list certain expenses in categories that are even more specific. Again, bear in mind the method and categories that will work best for your B&B.

Your Daily Tasks

Running a B&B, like any small business, requires that you be a good juggler and able to switch back and forth between a variety of tasks. A B&B is different from many other small businesses, however, since the tasks are so different and disparate. For instance, one minute you may be cooking a gourmet breakfast for your guests, and a half hour later you may be working with your accountant, while 15 minutes later, the local paper will send a reporter to do a story on your B&B. If you are unable to switch gears quickly, you should think about putting somebody else in charge of certain tasks.

The Typical Business Day described in Chapter 1 gives you a good idea of the variety of tasks you'll be called on to perform in the course of running your B&B each day. Some of the duties, however, won't be necessary each day; sometimes certain tasks get bunched up all on one day or during a certain period of the month or year. It's up to you to be prepared to handle them—or have someone else who can. And once you've run your B&B for a while, you'll start to develop a feel for the rhythm of the business and actually be able to anticipate some of the necessary tasks before they reach the Immediate Attention Requested stage.

Hiring Employees

Some B&B owners prefer to keep their operations small, specifically so they'll be able to handle all the jobs themselves without having to hire outside help. And with the rise in employee lawsuits brought as the result of being fired, many B&B owners have been further discouraged from hiring help. Hiring and managing employees adds a whole new dimension to your business and has both its good and bad points: For one, it means more paperwork because you'll have to pay state, federal, and perhaps local payroll taxes in addition to Social Security and worker's compensation, and, if you decide to offer it, insurance. On the other hand, having someone around to help out with the grunt work means you'll have more time to focus on running and building your business, like marketing and improving your B&B.

But unfortunately, a common complaint of business owners everywhere today is that it's hard to find good help; after all, no paid employee is going to regard your business and customers in the same meticulous and painstaking light that you will. So you'll probably have to lower your standards of quality and attention and plan to spend some time making up for the lack.

Many B&B owners advise that if you find an employee who is the exception to the rule, hold onto her as tightly as you can by increasing pay, offering bonuses, and expressing your appreciation with added responsibilities and the occasional day off with pay.

When hiring employees, there are certain things you have to know. If you're hiring a person to work for you regularly, cooking, cleaning, answering the phone, or greeting guests, he or she will be considered to be your employee and you will have to withhold income taxes, which you will file with the government either quarterly or once a year, depending on your tax setup.

Some businesses get around the process of withholding and payroll taxes by hiring an independent contractor. This way, the contractor files a self-employment tax, which saves you a lot of paperwork. This works for such seasonal and periodic workers as gardeners and musicians, but it will send up red flags with the IRS if you try to hire a part-time maid or office assistant in this way. The IRS has strict criteria for distinguishing an independent contractor from an employee, and this has been an area of abuse in small businesses. If you do hire an independent contractor, and pay them more than $600 over the course of a year, you must file a 1099 form, which reports their income.

No matter how you decide to staff your business, make sure that you always communicate clearly, directly, and immediately when there's a problem or complaint. And let people know when you think they did a job well.

Working with Suppliers

When you're first starting out, you'll probably buy your supplies—food, office equipment, and sheets—from stores and businesses you already have dealt with in the past. Later on, as you grow, you might want to deal directly with wholesalers and commercial distributors.

The first issue you'll face when approaching suppliers is meeting the large minimum orders that they usually require in order to keep their costs down. Their minimum might be more than you'll use in a month—or a year—and if you're dealing with perishable items, this is not feasible. When checking suppliers' prices, you might discover that their prices are actually higher than the supermarket, since they include the cost of delivering the supplies to you in their overhead. And, even for a distributor who deals in more than one type of supply, your combined potential order might be too small to interest the company.

If you're like most B&B owners, in the beginning you'll probably decide to buy retail, from food to new sheets. Some local businesses will allow you to set up a house charge account to simplify your bookkeeping and so that you can send a staff member to the market to pick up a few last-minute items and you don't have to dig up some cash and count the change you receive back. Some of these "suppliers" will also offer you a discount for buying in quantity and also for paying before net 30 days.

Even if you buy retail, however, it still pays to shop around. When buying office supplies, for instance, you'll probably spend the most at your neighborhood stationery store. The next cheapest source will be a stationery superstore, though sometimes the quality and attention you'll receive is far below what you're used to. In my experience, the cheapest source of office supplies are the mail-order operations that ship the same day your order is received and offer large discounts on top of their already low prices for volume orders.

There are exceptions to everything, however, so the best advice is to take your time, shop around and don't be afraid to dicker. These companies want your business, and if you show you're going to be a good, steady customer they'll work hard to keep you.

Understanding Taxes

When you first set up your B&B and discover how much time, energy, and paperwork you devote to taxes, you might wonder when you'll find the time to make breakfast and spend time with your guests. After payroll taxes, your income and other personal taxes, and the room and lodging tax, it can all seem pretty self-defeating. Why go into business if most of your revenue will go towards taxes?

First of all, take a deep breath. It only seems overwhelming now as you're learning about your different responsibilities. Once you get the hang of it, recording and paying taxes—as well as figuring out your deductions—will consume just a small part of your bookkeeping and office time. As I mentioned earlier, this is why it's important to keep good records.

Of course the tax rates vary from state to state, but in most states your guests will be required to pay a tax—called either a sales tax or a rooms and meals tax—on the amount paid for a night's stay at your B&B. Some B&Bs figure the tax into the room rate and state the tax is included, but it's not a good idea to do this. First, guests are used to the idea of paying a tax on travel expenses. But also, in some cases, rolling a tax into your basic room rate may alert the state tax commissioner to your practice and increase your chances of an audit, since it may seem that you're trying to hide some income from the state.

You will need to keep track of your revenue and expenses and pay taxes to the IRS on any profit your B&B earns. The amount of tax you pay will depend on the type of business you're running: a sole proprietorship or partnership, or a corporation. The tax structures for each differ.

Of course, since the start-up costs in a B&B are so high the first year or two, your expenses may even exceed your income, so you won't have to pay tax. The IRS allows that there will be years when you'll earn no profit on paper, even though it assumes you are in business to earn a profit. As a result, many businesses claim a wealth of deductions to avoid showing a profit, and therefore, paying tax. Current tax law says that you must show a profit at least three years out of five to prove that you are running a viable business. If you show a loss three or more years out of the five, again, this will alert the IRS and set up the possibility of an audit. In the early to mid '80s, before B&Bs caught on, the IRS and state and local tax collectors didn't know what to make of this new business, because it wasn't like a hotel and it wasn't like an inn, both of which are considered to be commercial entities that are in business in make a profit. B&Bs not only frequently didn't show a profit, but they operated out of the owner's home, and the deductions claimed by home businesses always catch the eye of the IRS.

Recently, as more tax officials have had experience dealing with B&Bs, regular and unnecessary attention has been relaxed somewhat.

As for payroll taxes, contact your state employment bureau about the exact deductions you should make for each employee and the federal tax bureau for information about income tax, Social Security, and other payroll taxes.

Action Guidelines

✔ Estimate in advance what it will cost each month to run your B&B.

✔ Develop a system that painlessly allows you to maintain accurate records.

✔ Set the prices for your rooms according to what other B&Bs in the area are charging.

✔ Pick cash accounting or accrual accounting as a way to set up your books.

✔ Be clear about the pros and cons of hiring employees for your B&B.

B&B Profile

Molly Newell
Broadview Farm Bed & Breakfast
St. Johnsbury, Vermont

The road that passes in front of the main house at Broadview Farm served as the Boston Post Road in the 19th century. The house was built in the early 1800s as a stagecoach inn on the route. Most B&Bs don't qualify for a spot on the National Historic Register, though it definitely is a selling point to guests if it does.

The reason most don't is that the restrictions are a little steep: A building makes it onto the prestigious list if 1) somebody famous owned it or slept there; 2) the building is particularly old, even for the area; or 3) its architecture is unusual for the area.

Broadview Farm made the list for the last reason. Molly Newell, who runs the B&B with her husband, Joe, learned that her grandfather bought the place in 1904. But a traditional farmhouse didn't suit him—he came from Newport, Rhode Island—so he added lots of Italianate arches, which are common in his native area. Then it felt more like home.

Molly's grandfather ran Broadview as a gentleman's farm, as did her parents, who bought the farm in 1957. Today Molly and Joe are following the tradition on their 309-acre homestead, concentrating on maple sugaring, selling Christmas trees and wreaths, and running a B&B. In fact, the bed-and-breakfast is open only from July through October, and in January and February—when there are lulls in the Newells' other businesses. These other businesses are of considerable size: the sugar grove has almost 2,000 taps, which Joe wants to increase to 3,500. "We already have requests for more syrup that we make," he says, which is up to 400 gallons a year. The farm's medium amber syrup was selected as the best in the state in 1992, and each guest receives a small jug of syrup to take home.

The four guest rooms upstairs are filled with the artifacts of the lives of Molly's relatives, and guests always ask a lot of questions about them. In what she calls the children's room, there's a picture of her father and his twin sister as children in front of the farmhouse. A pair of Molly's aunt's shoes hang above the bureau. In the Whittier room, named for her opera singer aunt, Harriet Whittier, a pair of old pointe shoes, silver brushes and combs rest on the table.

Guests visit with a golden retriever named Cooper and a cat named Florence. When Joe retired from the army in 1986, he and Molly moved to Broadview; they opened the B&B shortly after.

"We're doing exactly what we set out to do," she says.

Chapter
7

MARKETING

Marketing frequently makes many B&B owners uncomfortable. Marketing may conjure up images of expensive and ineffective ad campaigns as well as the feeling that there's something mystical about the ability to draw in customers on the strength of just words or pictures.

You don't need a degree in marketing to sell your business effectively. In fact, you're apt to sell it better than a professional because you're not doing what everyone else who's earned an expensive degree in marketing is doing. After all, you know your business best. And if you're thinking of hiring somebody else to do it just to get the job off your hands, forget about it. Just as no one else will handle your guests like you will, so too you're the best person to promote your B&B. After all, who else is better acquainted with the business and therefore better able to convey its value to others?

Marketing can actually be fun and as creative as artfully arranging a breakfast of orange pancakes with a fresh fruit garnish. In fact, the more creative you are, the better—for you and your B&B.

The Purpose of Marketing

You have a great product: your B&B. But how will anyone hear about it unless you tell them?

"Oh, they'll see the sign in front of the house," you'll reply. As with any ad or notice that publicizes your B&B, unfortunately only a tiny percentage of the people who pass by your B&B will respond by coming in and taking a room for the night.

"Well, what about the Chamber of Commerce? I'm a member, you know." Yes, and so are 300 other businesses in your town, all seeking the same thing you are—customers.

Joining the chamber of commerce or other local business organization is a great idea, but they'll only do so much for you. After all, their role is to promote area businesses as a group, and not individually.

"My brochure knocks 'em dead." But how are you going to get it in the hands of prospective guests in the first place? It's great if your brochure and other promotional materials really convey what it's like to stay at your B&B. However, prospective customers must first see the brochure at local businesses if they're already in the area, or when they're at home deciding where to spend a rare weekend away.

The purpose of marketing is to develop and execute a number of different strategies that result in first letting potential guests hear about your B&B, and then convincing them to give you a try. Admittedly, some guests will come to stay at your B&B when all other rooms within a 100-mile radius are taken. This is one reason why it's a good idea to join the local chamber of commerce and travel bureaus, because they know where to steer people who arrive without reservations on the busiest weekend of the year.

However, you must be proactive and devote time and creativity to the marketing plan you developed in Chapter 4. Always keep in mind that marketing in whatever form will help you to meet new customers—and bring back current customers. Repeat business is the lifeblood of any B&B, and the best thing about repeat guests, besides the friendships you'll cultivate, the fact that getting them back incurs little or no additional marketing costs. They're already convinced, and you don't have to sell them.

Defining Your Customers

B&B guests come in all stripes: young, old, singles, couples, and families. Most people pick a B&B because they enjoy the homeyness and intimacy they can't find at an impersonal chain hotel. No doubt with the rising popularity of B&Bs since the mid- to late '80s, you'll get some guests who've never stayed in a B&B before. Most likely one night at your B&B will make them instant converts, which again, results in more business for you and the B&B industry as a whole.

Americans are largely overwhelmed by media messages today. In addition, most of those messages have become quite specialized in addressing the advertiser's target audience.

You must do the same thing. You won't be able to reach everybody—and even if you could, your message is only one of thousands they see and hear every day. The first step to reaching your customers is to target the kind of guest you'd like to attract, even though a wider variety than you thought existed will eventually walk through your doors and sleep in your beds. Keeping individual records about your customers from the beginning can help you to define your customer even more once you've been in business for awhile.

Granted, the type of B&B you run, along with your location, and your pricing structure will help to determine the kinds of guests most likely to select your B&B. For example, a college student in town to catch an early connecting train is probably not going to want to stay at your B&B if you charge more than $50 for a night. Similarly, an elderly couple who wants to tour your town's historic district will pick your B&B if your rates are reasonable, you're within walking distance of the historic district, and you don't cater to single downhill skiers. Of course, there will be a continual crossover of people with different interests who will meet at your breakfast table and forge instant friendships, but the general rule is to first define your ideal customers and let the rest come as part of the wide net you cast.

Defining your customer means you can then narrow down your choice of the avenues you have available to reach them, as well as the methods you use.

Ask yourself the following questions:

- What are the three types of customers you'd like to reach? For example, urban couples away for a romantic weekend, parents visiting a child at a nearby private school, or skiers or mountain bikers?
- Where will your customers come from?
- What is the customers' income range? Are they urban professionals with discretionary income looking for real hospitality, or bohemian wanderers with limited income who eschew the conformity of chain hotels?
- Why will they stay at your B&B?
- How long will they stay?

Finding Prospects

You have an idea of the kinds of guests who will be attracted to your B&B. Now, how do you find them?

Through a variety of ways. You should know, however, that prospects are not the same thing as customers. In fact, only a small percentage of people who inquire about your B&B and ask for or pick up your brochure will actually spend a night in your B&B. You must view all prospects as potential customers, and callers like friends planning a visit, but do not be disappointed when they don't call back to make a reservation. We have become a society of fishermen: because there is so much out there to choose from, we must know all there is about everything there is before we make a decision. And even then, there's a little voice in the back of our heads that says, "There's always something better."

Perhaps that is true. But you can help find and convert prospects into paying customers by concentrating on those avenues that your group of defined customers travel.

For instance, do you plan to offer a romantic weekend for two package? Then contact the editor of the lifestyle section of your local newspaper, place a special brochure in local flower and gift shops, and take out an ad on the bridal page.

Do you want local corporations to book your entire B&B for executive retreats? Contact the meeting planners at the companies and let them know of your B&Bs availability, as well as assuring the participants' complete privacy at your B&B.

Are you targeting guests who live in a major city two hours away? Spend a couple days there, distributing brochures, doing radio and TV talk shows, or newspaper interviews. Contact and meet with the director of a local woman's club or some other social group a few weeks in advance to set up a luncheon talk about what it's like to run a B&B. At the end, pass out discount coupons inviting members of the audience to come spend a weekend at your B&B.

Got the idea? Marketing is not always advertising, as many people wrongly assume. In fact, advertising is one of the least effective and most expensive ways to find your prospects.

Think about your defined customers and then consider the places you can find them; use some of the above suggestions for a jumping-off point. You'll undoubtedly be able to think of many more.

Cloning and Keeping Good Customers

Once you get good customers, hold onto them. Tight. The good news is that your good customer knows other people who could also be good customers. After all, word of mouth is probably the most effective kind of marketing there is.

There are a variety of ways you can clone good customers. One way, if you send a regular letter or newsletter to repeat guests, is to ask them if they know of other people who would like to receive information about your B&B. Keep track of any reservations you receive through this referral system, because if a referral becomes a guest, you can offer the referring guest a discount on their next stay. One B&B sends a discount coupon for 10 percent off a two-night stay to frequent guests and encloses an identical coupon for the guest to give to a friend. Treating your repeat customers well each time they stay with you is in essence a kind of cloning, since they are likely to come back again and again.

Some B&Bs report that up to 80 percent of their business consists of guests who have already stayed with them. The best way to build up to this level and continue to clone other good customers is to continue to market to your targeted group of customers and be consistent in maintaining the quality of your B&B. After all, one of the reasons why guests return is because they know what to expect.

Finding the Time

Finding the time to market your business is one of the biggest problems that B&Bs have when it comes to marketing. The next time you say you don't have time to market your B&B, consider the words (on p. 117) from one innkeeper who sets aside time to market her business every day.

Then consider some of the following ideas whenever you complain that you lack the time to market.

- A lot of marketing involves grunt work: stuffing envelopes, making lists, shuffling through ad rate cards. Do this during slow times of the day or night; it's easier to justify when ten other things aren't demanding your attention.

- Examine your slow times, whether it's every Monday or the month of March. Use it to write your marketing plan, setting up the following year's strategies by writing your marketing plan (see Chapter 4). Then perform maintenance tasks on your weekly slow day.

"Time, of course, is the biggest marketing problem for B&B hosts and other small travel businesses. But if the owners would know how much business they could bring in, they might realize that some of the cooking and cleaning is best delegated to someone else, so they can make the time for serious marketing. To wit, here are the dollars we've billed in first-time business from recent national magazine coverage:

Country Living (two-page spread): $82,400 over the course of two years;

Yankee (13-page feature): $60,000 over the course of 18 months;

Country Home (eight-page feature): $23,300 over the course of 14 months.

Total: $165,700

"Because of these figures, it's imperative to ask each customer or potential customer *how you heard about us.* This information should then be tabulated to determine your rate of return on paid advertising and where to spend more of your valuable time and money. Seeing exactly what you have billed from each of the previous year's directories, ads, and listings makes the media-buying decisions much clearer. And it also becomes much easier to say no to pesky ad sales reps whose publications don't work for you."

- Survey your staff for ideas. If appropriate, let them carry them out with your approval. Pay for all expenses, and hold a monthly contest for the best idea. They may surprise you.

- Here's a sneaky tip: Ask sales reps from different media to design a media plan for you as a way to get your business. Many reps will do this anyway, of course, giving the biggest percentage of the pie to themselves. Whether you follow through is up to you, but you'll get lots of suggestions and ideas at no cost or time spent. Always ask about upcoming promotional tie-in events; frequently you'll get a reduced rate and increased exposure at the event as well.

- Hire someone to carry out your plan if you truly can't find enough time, or give the responsibility to a staff member. One outfitter hired a PR consultant who was just starting out. She paid the consultant a below-market rate but tied bonuses into any increased business that resulted from the additional publicity. Some travel business owners say that novices are better than experts; although they don't have the contacts, they also don't have a lot of preconceived notions about what's right and what's wrong. With marketing, innovation gets attention.

Advertising on a Budget

Advertising is a type of marketing where you pay for a certain amount of space or time so you can tell your message to a particular audience. Since you're paying to send the message, you can say anything you want—time or space and money are the only factors that limit you.

Considering these limitations, advertising doesn't really give you much leeway. In fact, because you bought the space you're obviously selling something, and most people turn right off when someone's trying to sell them something.

Take a look at the ads in your local newspaper or area magazine. What do they look like? How do they make you feel? Is there one in the entire publication that makes you want to drop what you're doing, pick up the phone and call?

Probably not. Do the same thing the next time you're watching TV or listening to the radio. Pay close attention to the locally produced ads. Again, do they make you feel excited about whatever it is the advertiser is trying to sell?

I probably can predict what your answer will be. The vast majority of advertising in all media is placed to gain consumer awareness, to let people know that a business exists. And this type of advertising can build business for a B&B—but very slowly. It's also hard to measure. How often do you go into a store and say that you heard their radio commercial? Unless the owner is a friend of yours, probably never.

Because advertising is so expensive, you can't waste money using it just to let people know you're there. Publicity and other more direct marketing tools exist for this reason, and they're also cheap.

No, the only reason you should spend money to advertise is to support a special promotion or discount available for a limited time; or to offer customers something for responding to your ad. A toll-free number, a discount coupon, or a special incentive will help you to measure how many people responded and reserved a room as the result of your ad. Then you can see if the ad paid for itself, and whether you should try another ad in a later issue of the magazine.

Some B&B owners report that they've felt pressure from a newspaper or magazine editor to advertise in exchange for a promise to cover their business in an editorial section of the publication. Though most editors will deny this ever happens, it does; and it's most likely to occur at smaller publications, where most or all of their revenue comes from advertising. And when the publisher also serves as the editor, you can be sure that any conflict of interest between advertising and editorial departments is frequently ignored.

If you do decide to advertise, don't settle for the quoted rate. Always ask, "Is that the best you can do?" Especially if the publication is nearing its closing date and there's still ad space left to fill, the sales rep or ad director might let it go at a significant discount; this is known as remnant space. In addition, radio and TV stations and publications frequently offer a special rate to first-time advertisers in the hopes that they'll become regular advertisers. At other times, they'll offer a discount if you advertise in a special section or sponsor a certain program. Again, you should always ask.

Radio and TV advertising don't usually work for B&Bs. Your primary audience consists of people who don't live in your area. Even if you were to advertise for guests in another area, it's too expensive and the audience is far too broad. It's best to focus on print ads in travel publications and other magazines and newspapers that your target audience reads.

B&B Directories and Magazines

In addition to magazines, you'll probably be approached by the sales reps for the following year's directories-cum-magazines that are published by the state, regional, county, or local travel and lodging associations. How do you sort them out? Which will pull best for you? Here are four ways to decide.

1. *Narrow your focus.* You don't *have* to be in all of them. This year, concentrate on promoting one aspect of your business through the directories and buy a listing or ad in the directory that will promote this angle most effectively, for instance, through a special category for outdoor activities or romantic inns.

2. *Target your audience.* It might elevate your ego to be in the city directory, but if you're a winery that's 50 miles away, you'd be better off with those that are closer to home. Most city tourists who make it to the outskirts are on bus tours with a predetermined schedule. Independent city tourists want to stay in the city. In this case, investing in the state

directory might make sense, since people who initially request information from the state tourism bureau by mail tend to be interested in the whole state. Your ad might help steer them towards you and your area.

3. *Where do most of your visitors come from?* If you get a lot of referrals from the local chamber of commerce, take out a bigger listing in their directory to get even more.

4. *Other opportunities with the directory publisher.* If the association that publishes the directory sponsors a contest, offer a prize in exchange for a larger listing in the directory. Then tell them you'll help promote the contest through mailings to your own in-house list, enclosing fliers, or jotting a note about it in your letters to past and potential guests.

Publicity

In the opinion of many B&B owners, publicity is the best kind of marketing there is, for aside from the initial costs of preparing a press release and contacting the media about your B&B, publicity is free. And because when your B&B receives coverage in a magazine, newspaper, on radio, or TV, it is considered to be an endorsement of your business. You didn't pay someone to be mentioned, and the audience will respond more favorably to an unsolicited endorsement than to a paid ad.

An insider tip—editors, writers and reporters will rarely give a bad review to a B&B. First off, they don't have the space, and they don't want to waste their audience's time. So, in most cases, if you see a place written up in a travel magazine, it's likely that the editor has weeded out less spectacular places in order to write about the ones chosen.

As with defining your customer, you must also narrow down the media you wish to reach. Many times, your defined customer will select your media for you. For instance, if your ideal guests have professional careers and live in a large city two hours from your B&B, you should target the media they're likely to read or listen to. For instance, many city magazines published independently and the Sunday magazines of many newspapers have a regular travel section that reviews destinations that are usually within a reasonable drive of the publication's area of coverage. Check the name of the editor on the masthead, or the writer of the travel stories. Never contact the editor-in-chief of a large or frequent publication, since they are far too busy to respond. The managing editor or an associate editor is a far better choice. Or you can contact the writer whose byline regularly appears on travel stories.

In any case, you will need to send your media contact your brochure, any other pertinent information, copies of other stories about you and your B&B, a cover letter, and press release.

A cover letter should be short and to the point, and casual in tone. It also helps if you show you're familiar with the publication and the writer's work by mentioning a recent story. Try to highlight one feature that makes your B&B different from other B&Bs in your area. After all, the editor probably gets bombarded with mailings from B&Bs every day; his attitude about yours is probably going to be, "So what?"

Figure 7.1 is one sample cover letter. Adapt it to fit your needs.

It's also a good idea to offer an angle for a story where the editor could fit you in. Note that the owner of My Place didn't specifically ask that the writer include her B&B in any story. This appeals to editors and writers who get offers of complimentary lodging, meals, and admission to local attractions all the time. Offering travel writers and editors free accommodations is a mainstay of the business. Except for large metropolitan travel magazines and newspapers that have a no-free-trip policy in place, the majority of publications still publish articles based on complimentary press trips. Those publications that don't publish articles based on free trips think that this

Dear Travel Writer:

I am the owner of My Place B&B. Enclosed is a brochure, rate card, and an article that the local paper published about the unusual breakfasts we serve at My Place.

I thought you'd like to know about My Place, since I read your recent article about Their Place, two hours south of you. We're two hours north.

The next time you're planning a story on this area, give me a call. I'd be glad to fill you in about the little-known attractions that visitors don't often hear about.

Sincerely,

Mary Myplace

Figure 7.1: Publicity Cover Letter.

will cause a writer to overlook certain flaws that would concern a paying customer. The controversy is far from over.

Speaking of newspapers, and newspaper travel editors in particular, some of the most overworked, underpaid, and rude people are in this business. When travel writers send out query letters—maybe about *you*—they often complain that they hardly ever hear back from newspaper travel editors. Newspaper travel editors get this way because they are usually responsible for filling the same amount of space in a week that a magazine editor gets a whole month to luxuriate over. As a result, many smaller papers rely on wire services for bland copy that doesn't have much to do with their readers.

So don't just send a brochure and rate card. Tailor your letter to the editor and paper. Mention any recent guests who live in the editor's area, and tell about the special things they did. *This* will get the editor's attention.

And speaking of travel writers . . . a caveat. If a writer is on the staff at a particular publication, you can rest assured that the publication will probably do a story on your B&B in the near future, or at least mention your business within the context of an upcoming story. The editor or writer will probably not take the time—especially if it's on company-paid time—to take a trip unless he or she was sure that the magazine could use a story that would require the reporter to travel to your B&B. With freelancers who have no specific affiliation, however, it's your call.

Some freelance writers make their living from travel writing. Therefore, these writers most often request free accommodations. Because pay rates are so low—most newspaper travel sections pay $100 for a story in the Sunday paper, while smaller magazines pay an average of $300-$500—in my experience, professional travel writers are going to try to get as much mileage out of a stay at your B&B as possible. This means that the writer may place the same story in as many as twenty different magazines and newspapers throughout the country, in addition to including your B&B in a book or two.

A Travel Writer's Perspective

Barbara Radcliffe Rogers of Richmond, New Hampshire, with her husband, Stillman Rogers, has written seven travel guides. As she conducts her research, Rogers frequently stays in B&Bs and considers them for inclusion in the book she's currently working on.

Here, she talks about what she looks for in a B&B, and what makes her think twice about including it in her travel guides.

"I look for the way I'm greeted by the host. Does my arrival seem like it's the most important part of their day, or do I get the impression that they think I'm a damned nuisance? The personality of the host really makes the biggest difference in how I consider their B&B, because what sets B&Bs apart from other kinds of lodging is the warmth of the host and hostess. And I'm not just talking about when I first arrive at a place, but also throughout my stay. For instance, do they ask if I need suggestions of where to go to dinner or what to see? At one B&B, when we arrived in the afternoon, the hostess had fresh-baked cookies on the table to greet us. It's the little touches that tell me about the B&B hosts and sets the tone for my stay. I notice that before I notice anything else.

"My husband looks for consistent decor, even if it's eclectic. For example, are the decor and furnishings on the same taste level as the rest of the place, or does it look like early junk shop just jumbled together? The furniture and knickknacks could be from 50 different places, but it shouldn't look as if they were thrown into the room just because that room needed a bureau.

"He also likes a breakfast room that's cheery and bright. There's nothing drearier than coming down to breakfast and eating in a dark room. Regarding cleanliness, I don't really care if there are dust kitties under the furniture, but grout in the shower chipping off, that is another story. That goes beyond cleanliness, and reveals the lack of attention to the little details of upkeep.

"Once, we walked into a really nice B&B, and the owners had obviously had cabbage for dinner, and the place just stunk. The smell hit us in the face as we walked in the front door and it crept up into our room, and we thought maybe our clothes would smell like cabbage. The next morning it was fine, but if hosts are going to eat something like that, they should use a vent. Smells greet people immediately, and they put guests in either a good or bad frame of mind about a place. For that matter, I also don't like rooms that smell stale or smoky. Also, the potpourris with artificial oils can be pretty cloying.

"Another feature we look at are the beds: are they comfortable, are they firm, and do they squeak? One time the four of us—me, my husband, and two daughters—were jammed into a B&B, and the bed squeaked so badly, that every time somebody turned over everybody woke up. That's something that the owners of a B&B wouldn't notice unless they slept in it themselves.

"I like lots of personal details, like an apple on the bed-stand, or a little basket of cookies in each room. I'd rather have that than a chocolate. Also, please have some magazines besides *Country Living!* I also appreciate some local travel information, particularly on the little-known things around town. But I don't need somebody in Franconia Notch, New Hampshire, telling me that the Old Man in the Mountain is there. I like it when somebody tells me that it's Thursday night and they do old car cruises at the local drive-in, or that the historical society is only open once a week on Sunday afternoon, and they've got some neat stuff. Of course, hosts have to be prepared if people ask, so it helps to know about these things and to provide some tourist brochures at the desk.

"It's also nice to have somebody just give me some sort of attention besides, 'Here's your room, here's your key, we close at 10.' I look for some personality in a place, in how it's decorated, and in the innkeepers. The place should have something about it that makes me remember it the next year, where I can say that a particular B&B was really a neat place, and we did *this* there.

"I know that some of these things I'm talking about we can't really mention in our books. They don't show up in our writing, but they do color what we have to say about a particular B&B.

"My advice to aspiring B&B hosts is don't take on more than you can handle. Of course, it all looks easy in the beginning, and you don't know what you can and cannot handle until you actually start, but it's important to think about this. New B&B hosts come in and say they're going to redecorate this room and revamp that room and change the menu, but then they get so caught up in running the business, it takes all their time so they don't have anything left over for anything else. So don't start tearing things apart; don't take out all the lighting fixtures at once, do one room at a time. Don't try something major that's going to affect the whole place if you can possibly help it.

"When you first look at a B&B that you're considering buying, look at it very carefully, because those first impressions are going to influence you. It's very hard to look at a place with a fresh eye. I'd try to invite a travel writer to come and be brutally honest. You never see your own place the way a stranger sees it. It's like walking into your own house; it smells like your house, but other people aren't familiar with it.

"And for God's sake, have something other than Lipton tea bags or herb teas at breakfast. People like me who drink tea at breakfast would love to have English Breakfast tea. On a similar note, it's a good idea to ask guests the night before what they want if you don't usually have regular and decaf coffee already made. We've come down to breakfast at B&Bs where they only had regular coffee, and we don't drink it. So they had to rush back and boil water for me and make a pot of decaf for my husband. It would be nice if they asked the night before."

Other writers are just looking for a free ride. If you have your doubts, ask the writer if he's actively pursuing an assignment and with which magazines. Even though the money you spend to host the writer will be negligible, you don't want to be ripped off, either. It's up to you to decide if the writer is serious and sincere, and if so, if you think a possible mention in that particular magazine would be worth it to you.

Even so, a staff writer that you host may be on the verge of leaving the magazine, or else the magazine may not survive long enough to print your story. And the freelance writer with no major credits may strike it big with a story in a major magazine featuring your business because you chose to give her a chance.

In any case, just remember there are no guarantees, but the payoffs can be huge. As stated earlier, one B&B owner reports that a two-page spread in *Country Living Magazine* has brought in $82,400 in business over the course of two years, a 13-page feature in *Yankee* attracted $60,000 worth of business, and a story in *Country Home* has grossed $23,300.

Guidebooks

Go to the travel section of your local bookstore, and try not to be shocked by the sheer number of B&B and inn guidebooks. And those that are on the shelf are but a fraction of the total number. Books on B&Bs that appeal to families, singles, gays, Christians, nonsmokers, motorcyclists, and gourmets are just a few of the categories. In addition, these books can cover the entire country, a region, one state, or just a city.

Now get ready for another shock: most of these guidebooks charge each B&B to be listed in the book. The fees can range from a modest $25 for a one-paragraph description plus your address and phone number all the way up to $400 or more for a full-page listing, a line drawing of your B&B, and glowing accolades from guests.

There are also those that don't charge. These tend to include the travel guides that don't specifically focus on B&Bs,

but cover a wide range of places of interest to tourists within a certain theme or region.

There are some B&B owners who try to get in as many guidebooks as possible, no matter what the charge or audience, while there are others who refuse to pay anything to any publisher, believing that their B&B is worthy enough to be written up without payment. Most B&B hosts fall somewhere in the middle: they pay to be in a few guidebooks, after finding out which ones work best for them, and then work to get listed in the others. I've found that most B&B hosts who are just starting out pay to be in as many guidebooks as possible, and then discontinue their listings in the guides that don't pull. Most books are updated regularly; so keep in mind it might take a couple of years to get listed in one in the first place.

And some guidebooks pull much better than others. In New England, for instance, every B&B host I've spoken to who's been written up in author Bernice Chesler's *Bed & Breakfast in New England* (Globe Pequot) has reported that the response has been phenomenal, despite an inclusion fee of $125. The business they've received as a result of the listing has exceeded the fee many times over. Ask other B&B owners in your area which guidebooks bring in the best business for them.

Reservation Service

A B&B reservation service acts as a clearinghouse for your business. These mostly regional agencies may handle anywhere from 25 to 100 different B&Bs in a given area, in addition to possibly running their own as well. Here's how it works.

The service markets the fact that it represents many different kinds of B&Bs in a given area. A tourist who is looking to stay in a B&B in the area will call up and tell the agency reservationist the desired type of B&B, the location, the number of nights, and any other pertinent information like allergies or a desire to not have to climb any stairs.

The agency will check these specifics against the B&Bs on its roster, as well as the availability of rooms on the guest's desired dates, and then book the stay with the B&B. The agency will then send information to the guest—such as directions and a description of the B&B—who will pay the room rates directly to the agency, either with a credit card number over the phone or a check in the mail. The agency will then send it on to the B&B, minus a commission that can range from 15 percent to 33 percent.

What does the B&B owner get in return for this hefty fee? The agency serves as a screening bureau of sorts; the questions the booking agent asks virtually insures that the tourist will be matched to a B&B that meets every need. The agency also does all of the promotion and marketing work—finding potential guests and promoting the service—as well as all of the paperwork, which allows the B&B owner to leave many of the business details to someone else.

The drawbacks? With up to 100 other B&Bs to book guests into, some member B&Bs rarely see a guest, especially if they're in a less desirable location. Most agencies will screen a B&B before accepting them onto their roster. The agency is in business to make money and wants to make guests happy so they'll return, which means more money for the both of you.

In turn, some agencies will request that you do business strictly with them and do no marketing of your own since that would, in essence, put you in direct competition with the agency. For B&B owners for whom the business will remain mostly a sideline business, signing on with a reservation agency makes sense. But for those who want to grow their business into much more than an avocation, using a reservation agency should be only one tool in your overall marketing program.

Promotional Materials

Your brochure is the most important part of your marketing arsenal. Many times, it will be the first impression that a prospective guest has about your B&B. As such, it has the potential to make or break your business. And once you're set on the design for your brochure, all of your other promotional materials—stationery and business cards—should follow the same theme and look.

Basically, your brochure should consist of these ingredients:

- Description of the B&B
- Map and directions
- A detailed description of your rooms, especially if they each have a name and specific theme
- A photograph or line drawing of your B&B
- Local attractions and seasonal activities in your area
- Your name, address, and phone number, and fax if applicable
- Your reservation and cancellation policies
- Your price list

Some B&B hosts prefer to print these last two items on a separate sheet of paper to insert into the body of the brochure. This allows for annual and seasonal fluctuations, since many B&Bs normally print up 5,000 or 10,000 brochures at a time to save money; this quantity of brochures could last several years, depending upon your business and area. Printing the reservation and cancellation policies on a separate slip of paper allows all of the business part to be segregated from the fantasy side of why people want to come to your B&B; some B&B hosts feel that printing this information directly on the brochure distracts a guest from anticipating the experience he'll have at your B&B. It's basically up to you.

Since most B&Bs are more casual than either a larger country inn or a resort or small hotel, their brochures tend to be simpler, with one color of ink on textured ivory or cream-colored paper, and not glossy brochures with a number of four-color photos, like the big guys do—and can afford. That's why you'll find a lot of line drawings in B&B brochures. Besides, they tend to show your house at its best, without telephone wires and tree branches in the way.

Following are several examples of well-designed brochures for a variety of B&Bs. Note the different uses of type and design conveying a sense of the B&B itself. Format also plays a part in the overall design: one uses a notecard format (Figure 7.4, p. 135), which is appropriate for a B&B where the theme is good literature, while the other is a bookmark (Figure 7.5, p. 136), which is a marketing tool that more B&Bs might employ. The bookmark even includes a recipe for one of the breakfast specialties. Also notice the variety of names: historical, geographical, and thematic.

Beyond Your Traditional Markets

When you start your B&B, most of your guests will come because they saw your ad, brochure, or a story in the local paper; or they're visiting a relative in town who doesn't have a place for them to stay. When you book a guest who hasn't come to you through your normal marketing routes—advertising, publicity, brochures at the information booth—it can almost seem like found money.

Great, you think, I'm having enough trouble finding the time to do marketing at all, and now I have to go hunting for business in *other* places as well?

Don't worry; these other places are just as easy and inexpensive to pursue. In fact, they're even cheaper with a higher rate of return on your investment of time and money, simply because most other businesses won't go after them. So you'll be the standout.

Figure 7.2: Pine Crest B&B brochure.

Figure 7.3: The Woods House B&B Inn brochure.

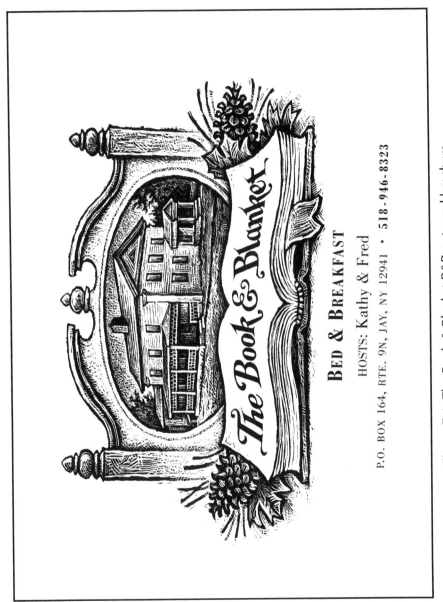

Figure 7.4: The Book & Blanket B&B notecard brochure.

Figure 7.5: Dutch Valley Heritage Inn B&B bookmark.

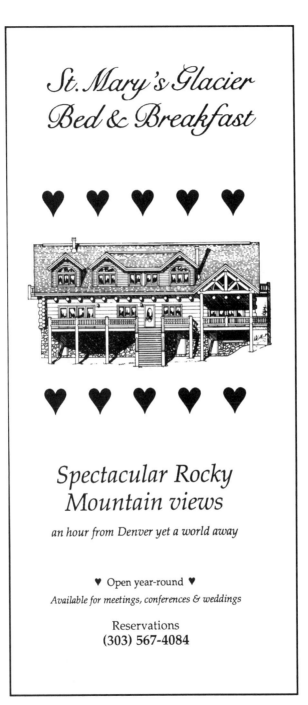

Figure 7.6: St. Mary's Glacier B&B brochure.

BROADVIEW FARM

Bed & Breakfast

Joe & Molly Newell, Innkeepers
Danville, Vermont
(802) 748-9902

**Listed in
the National Register
of Historic Homes**

Figure 7.7: Broadview Farm B&B brochure.

Sinclair Inn

Bed & Breakfast
R. D. #2, Box 35
Underhill, Vermont 05489

802/899-2234

We invite you to take a step back in time and capture the mood and charm of the Victorian era at Sinclair Inn.

formerly Sinclair Towers

Figure 7.8: Sinclair Inn B&B brochure.

Here they are. And don't be shy.

1. *Donate your B&B for a one-day outing to local nonprofit groups.* Frequently, nonprofit groups host out-of-town guests who need a place to stay; or these groups maybe looking for a special event to impress visitors. They tend to remember largesse, and it'll cost you next to nothing.

2. *Church groups and women's clubs are always looking for speakers for monthly meetings; volunteer!* Your best bet is to arrange to speak at a club luncheon in a city that tends to bring you lots of business. The topic? What it's like to run your business. Hand out your brochure with a discount coupon applicable towards their visit.

3. *Make your facility available to businesses for meetings and conferences.* Let area businesses know that your B&B is available for meetings, retreats, and seminars. This could be a nice fill-in business during the slow times. Local business people will also be more apt to recommend your facility to their out-of-town guests or clients.

4. *Canvass the engagement notices in the newspaper every week.* Some might think this practice to be comparable to reading the obits in a city where good apartments are at a premium, but it's a great idea if you want wedding business. Send a personalized letter offering reduced rates for lodging, catering, and a special package for the bride and groom. If they book with you, offer a free first-anniversary stay.

5. *Advertise in a place where you've never seen a business like yours advertise before.* But make it a classified with a knockout headline. Two places that come to mind are the back pages of the Boston *Phoenix* and New York's *Village Voice*, which are nothing *but* classified ads. Offer a special weekend or one-day event tied in with the season, and arrange for easy transportation out of the city.

6. *Don't overlook group tour operators.* I can tell you in advance that getting group tour operators to pay attention to your

B&B can be a tough nut to crack, but once you're in and a regularly-scheduled part of the tour, whether for an hour or an overnight, your reputation and bottom line will grow. Group tour operators run mostly extended bus tours; however, some tours can last a day or less and be geared toward locals and not tourists. First call the operator's office and ask for a catalog to get an idea of their focus. Find out where the operator's current tours run, and what their target market is. Ask if they're planning to expand to other areas in the future. Offer to serve as their contact for your area. Keep in touch, and regularly send them news of new services and attractions in your area. Suggest itineraries that you have developed for your guests, and send maps and brochures.

Another sideline is to make friends with your local step-on guides as a way to reach the operators. Step-on guides are hired by the tour operator to provide an in-depth tour of a locale; they are particularly valued for niche or historical tours. If you don't know who they are, contact your local chamber of commerce or tourist association for names and numbers.

The 14 Most Commonly Asked Marketing Questions

1. *Should I give something to a guest who refers another guest to me?*
A: Guests are going to refer other guests whether there's something in it for them or not. However, if you go out of your way to thank them with a handwritten note after the referral's departure, they'll remember you in the future with more referrals and increased bookings.

2. *I want to try a booth at a local consumer travel show, but I can't afford the booth rentals.*
A: Travel show promoters frequently say if you get just one or two extra bookings from the show, you will have paid for

the show fee and your travel expenses. That may be true, but once there, you have to take a proactive stance. Actually solicit people, answer their questions, invite them to call later with other concerns. Travel shows give you a rare chance to interact face to face with your best prospects. Also, many small travel businesses pool their resources and share a booth.

3. *How should I deal with freelance travel writers?*

A: Some small travel businesses provide a tour to all writers and a complimentary trip or overnight only in the case of a firm assignment. Others will provide familiarization trips and free accommodations to any writer with a travel credit. Freelancers will frequently write about the same subject for a variety of publications, increasing your chances for even more exposure. If in doubt, ask to see their clips or a copy of their contract, though this may turn the bona fide writers off. When I was researching my farm vacation book, which was contracted and scheduled, one innkeeper sent me a letter saying I was welcome to tour the inn but not to stay overnight. He added that when a fabulous review came out, only then would the inn would provide a complimentary stay. Since I won't write up a destination unless I can experience it through a guest's eyes, I said forget it. Needless to say, that inn did *not* appear in the book.

4. *What kind of photographs should I have on hand?*

A: Photographs that are in focus are rarer than you might think, but you don't need a professional photographer for publishable pictures. If you run guided trips or a tourist attraction, make sure your pictures contain smiling people who are in the act of enjoying the services you offer. For an inn or small hotel, a head-on exterior shot along with a well-lit interior photo is essential.

5. *How do I track which ads pull?*

A: Most businesses ask new prospects where they heard about their company, but frequently people will give the name of a wrong magazine—or one that doesn't even exist. Classify each ad and article with its own department number and track your responses. Then gear your future advertising and publicity plans towards those markets that pull best.

6. *Marketing is my Achilles heel. I know I should do it, but I'm not sure how to go about it. What can I do?*

A: Marketing is a scary thing for many people, but if you spend an uninterrupted period of time each week just on marketing, your business will grow. Either set aside a five-hour period once a week—and hire someone to answer the phone for the afternoon—or set a goal to accomplish one marketing task each day. For instance, send out letters to five people who have just completed a trip or a visit, thanking them; or send notes and information to five different editors, writers, or producers.

7. *I think my business appeals mostly to women. How do I target them?*

A: Gear your promotional material toward the market you want to reach. Then market your business towards two audiences: the general and the specific. General marketing will reach members of your desired audience who don't read specialized publications. The specific markets are smaller, but in most cases, they're more responsive to your message. And the fact that you're marketing toward women has a real benefit: One rule in marketing, from bike trips to inns, is if you reach the women, the family will follow. Give talks to women's groups and offer press trips to editors at women's and family publications.

8. *Help! What do I do when the media calls?*

A: Drop everything and smile. Treat them like royalty while you make it appear like it's business as usual.

9. *How can I increase my off-season business?*

A: Special events, business and convention meetings, and promoting to targeted groups is the way to go to even out your year. Mystery weekends and chocolate festivals have worked well, as have women-only adventure travel weeks and discounts aimed towards people who live in your community. Many Vermont ski areas offer discounted midweek lift tickets to Vermont and New Hampshire residents.

10. *How do I set my marketing budget as a percentage of total sales?*

A: Customarily, businesses should set aside anywhere from 5 percent to 25 percent of gross sales to invest in marketing and promotion. For small travel businesses, however, even 5 percent can be too much. Instead, you should put the bulk of your limited energies and dollars into creative, inexpensive marketing strategies like publicity. One tourist-oriented gift shop in eastern Pennsylvania held a Clean Sweep sale where each customer who brought in a broom received 20% off their purchases. Valet broom parking was provided, and some customers even bought a broom just for the sale. There was a line out the door, the event was written up in the newspaper, and local business also picked up as a result.

11. *How come the same travel companies get written up in the big magazines?*

A: These inns, outfitters, and tourism associations spend a good deal of time cultivating their media contacts. Even if a reporter just calls for a brochure, the person in charge of marketing adds them to the media list and regularly sends out personalized notes about new features or programs. And an open invitation is a given.

12. *How can I light a fire under our local chamber of commerce?*

A: Be a pest. One new B&B host brought a basket of fresh-baked muffins to the town's chamber of commerce every day for a month during the height of tourist season. He attached a card with the name of his B&B and his address and phone number to the basket. When tourists came into the office for recommendations, they ate the muffins, saw the card, and asked the director about it, who also ate her fair share of muffins. The B&B was booked at close to capacity for the entire season.

13. *Can I really negotiate for better ad rates off the rate card?*

A: Yes, especially if the issue closing date is nearing and there's still empty space to fill. Ask the ad director for special rates for new advertisers, frequency discounts, cheaper special sections and if you can delay your payment until the issue goes to press. It *is* possible to save up to 75 percent on advertising. Most people simply don't ask, and end up paying full price.

14. *Do radio interviews work?*

A: For lodging businesses, radio interviews increase your local visibility so that people nearby can recommend you to their out-of-town guests. But overall, I feel that local radio does more for your ego than your bottom line.

Don't Let this Happen to You

Following is the problem, analysis, and solution for a B&B that fell into a rut.

The Business: A rural Midwest B&B with five rooms. It's open year-round, and summer is their busiest season. Local attractions include golf, hiking, and a university town 15 miles away.

Current Marketing Strategy: Every spring, the B&B owner sends his new brochure to his in-house list, takes out a one-inch reader-response display ad in his local regional lifestyle magazine, and has a steady number of referrals. He doesn't do any publicity, saying the results don't justify the expense and time. Less than 1 percent of his new prospects turn into paying guests, and response from his in-house list shrinks each year. He farms out the brochure work to a local graphic artist who simply pulls up last year's catalog and plugs in new dates and prices.

The Problem: The owner has been running the company for 5 years and is burned out. He spends more time in the office than conversing with guests, which is the main reason why he began the company. And his overall numbers are stagnating.

The Solution: The business has fallen into a big rut, caused by the owner's impending burn-out. He should give the marketing work to a staff member who has some new ideas, and get a new designer to shake up his brochure. No wonder his house list isn't responding—his brochure is far too predictable.

He might think about hiring a freelance publicity specialist to write releases, target a media list, and make follow-up calls, if he finds the work too distasteful. True, some editors are rude to people who call to follow up on press mailings, and it may sometimes seem like his mailings fell into a dark abyss, but just because someone has her name on the masthead of a magazine does not turn her into a god. He should keep this in mind whenever he deals with the media.

And although publicity is the bane of many B&Bs, it's the best and cheapest way to keep your name out there. And when he hits it right—which is due to a combination of skill, positioning, timing, and luck—he'll probably hit it big. He should draw up a wish list of magazines and newspapers—local and national—that he'd like to appear in, and then figure out the best way to approach each of them. He might have to write a letter with a different angle for each editor and reporter.

Another idea is to add some off-season events. It's hard for a B&B to get a lot of repeat business if he doesn't offer something new each year. To convert more of the first-time prospects from the magazine responses, he should offer a special deal to them, like taking 5 percent or 10 percent off if they sign up by a certain date of if they book with a friend, or perhaps offering a free cookbook or regional inn guidebook. If the guest doesn't book within a month of receiving the brochure, the owner or a staff member should call her up and ask what would make her register. He should listen carefully and file their words away, because it will help in planning future trips and marketing strategies.

Action Guidelines

✔ Analyze the types of customers you'd like to reach.

✔ Think about the places you're most likely to find them.

✔ Continually market to guests who have already stayed with you at least once.

✔ Don't consider advertising to be your only form of marketing.

✔ Be cordial but not overly fawning when dealing with travel writers and editors.

✔ In the beginning, it's a hit-or-miss prospect discovering which guidebooks will work best to attract guests to your B&B.

✔ Consider the pros and cons of signing up with a reservation agency, as well as any restrictions they will place on you.

B&B Profile

Mary Shaw
Bed & Breakfast/Chicago, Inc.

Back in the early '80s, Mary Shaw was looking for a business to buy or start. She was living in Chicago with two small children, had spent most of her career working in the corporate world, and was looking for a change. She had read about a bed-and-breakfast reservation service that was operating primarily in the suburban North Shore area of the city and thought that becoming a B&B host was the kind of business she was looking for. Little did she know that within a year, not only would her B&B be a huge success, but that she'd be running the agency as well.

After six months of being a host, she asked the owners if she could buy into the agency. One sold Shaw her share, and within the year, the other had sold out as well. Today, Shaw still runs her own B&B, which is really a self-contained apartment in her townhouse in the Old Town section of Chicago, in addition to the agency, with 70 hosts all over the city and about 50 of them active.

Shaw feels that signing on with an agency is the only way for urban B&Bs to go. "I protect my hosts," she says. "Guests don't receive the address to a B&B until it's booked. In the city especially, there are a lot of crazies, and I perform a lot of screening. After all this time, I'm good at getting a certain feel about a person, and usually err on the side of turning people away."

She adds that if you run a B&B without an agency, you run the risk of having people show up on your doorstep at all hours. However, if her hosts also want to market themselves without the agency, she doesn't mind. But many of them end up coming back to her exclusively. "My hosts who have marketed their

B&Bs independently always have more trouble with their guests," says Shaw. "Maybe because of the way I work with many different kinds of B&Bs, I can see things more objectively and describe them that way to make a better match."

What does she look for in B&B owners who want to sign up with her agency? Through a number of preliminary and final visits to prospective B&Bs, Shaw looks first for cleanliness, which she says is a totally nonnegotiable aspect to her B&Bs. "I also look for a good attitude in my hosts and stylishness in the B&B. I do have certain hosts who are completely stylish but are also pretty cold fish, but there are certain guests for whom that would work," she says. "I always try to ferret out on the phone what they're looking for. After all, that's my job, to make sure the match is correct."

Why does she turn certain B&Bs down? When a prospective host calls, Mary sends them an information packet that explains what's needed and what guests expect. After the host indicates that she's interested, Mary will then set up an appointment to view the B&B, and she'll get there and know immediately it won't work. Why? "I'll get there and the closets are not cleaned out, and it's not ready to go," she says. "Also, in some cases, the layout is screwy, like you have to walk through a living room to get to the bathroom. That makes many guests uncomfortable."

Most of her host B&Bs have only one room, and Shaw keeps them pretty busy. "If a host is a good host, gets good feedback and is centrally located, I'll tell them I'll barely let their beds cool off," she says.

Bed & Breakfast/Chicago earns a 25 percent commission on a daily basis for most of the guests she books into B&Bs. The rates for double occupancy can range from $55 to $75 a night, and the apartments on her roster are priced from $75 to $150 a night. Both require a two-night minimum. For longer bookings, Mary will lower her commission.

Sometimes, a guest will be unhappy with her accommodations; Mary takes the position that the customer is always right, and she responds appropriately. "I give away a lot of free rooms and offer my apologies," she says. "I have a three-strikes-and-you're-out policy with my hosts, and try to stay away from the he-said, she-said stuff."

Another characteristic she looks for in her hosts is someone who's not just in the business for the money, because with only one room, her hosts don't expect to make a living from it. "They should see their B&B as the icing on the cake, because it will bring lots of interesting people into their lives and will add another dimension to it. And that's the difference between a hotel and a B&B: With a hotel, you feel like you're passing through a place. With a B&B, you feel like you're part of the place."

Chapter

8

FINANCES

I recently spoke with a B&B host who had bought her business the previous year from a husband and wife who had
owned the B&B for 10 years.

The previous owners had sold the B&B because they were
burned out, and it showed, in the worn carpets, rickety old
furniture, and outdated brochure.

But that wasn't all. "She never kept any financial records at
all," the new owner told me. And so, before buying the business, the new owner had to go through all of the B&B's reservation books and the rate sheets to determine the business's
annual income, and dig through 10 years of pay stubs and
canceled checks to figure out the B&B's expenses. She says it
only took a few days, but I figure after a short time, she got
sick of it and just averaged costs and revenue for each year.

"I'm the type to keep records," the new owner said, shak-
ing her head. "I don't know *how* they did it."

Fortunately, she was able to piece together a financial picture of the business. Many B&Bs just guess when it comes to
taxes, profit-and-loss statements, and cash flow. And if they
ever want to sell the business, well, you see what happens
when the prospective buyer wants to get an idea of the B&B's
financial health.

It's not too difficult to keep a handle on the various financial aspects of running your B&B. Take some time with it now, and you'll spend less down the road.

Profits and Losses

One important way to gauge how your business is doing is to prepare a profit and loss statement. Even though money may be coming in regularly through room revenue, it may be possible that you are losing money because your expenses exceed your income.

Keeping accurate records will help make preparing a profit and loss statement much easier; all you have to do is plug in the numbers. There are two kinds of profit and loss statements you can keep: one that projects your estimated profits and losses, and another that tracks actual figures on a weekly or monthly basis to help you see how well your B&B is doing. You can also compare the two, and if your projections are either 20 percent higher or lower than your actual figures, based on seasonality, you can adjust your projected profit and loss statements accordingly.

With a B&B, it's sometimes difficult to accurately figure expenses, since some of your personal expenses, like food, the mortgage, and utilities will be included in the B&B's expenses. The good thing about running a B&B as your main source of revenue is that most of the expenses you'll incur in connection with the house will be deductible. Your share of the food, for example, will be negligible in comparison with the total costs, and so you'll be able to deduct most, if not all, of your expenses.

To figure out your profit and loss statement for your B&B, you must first calculate the number of guest nights per year, estimate your occupancy rate—or else base it on the previous owner's figures—figure the gross income, and then deduct your expenses.

A simple case would be a four-room B&B open year round. Three of the rooms cost $60 a night, while the fourth costs $50.

The total number of possible guest nights would be 1,460 or 4 rooms x 365 days. Because the rooms are priced differently, however, it's a good idea to calculate occupancy rates on the two differently-priced rooms that are available.

Say that the occupancy rate on the three $60-rooms is about 40%; your gross revenue would be:

> 3 rooms x 365 days = 1,095 guest nights
> 1,095 guest nights x $60 = $65,700
> $65,700 x 40% occupancy = $26,280

The $50 room occupancy rate is only 30 percent, resulting in a gross revenue of $5,475.

> 1 room x 365 days = 365 guest nights
> 365 guest nights x $50 = $18,250
> $18,250 x 30% occupancy = $5,475

The total gross revenue, based on the existing vacancy rates, is $31,755.

> $26,280 + $5,475 = $31,755

If you were fully booked every night of the year, your gross would be $83,950.

> $65,700 + $18,250 = $83,950

As you can see, running a small B&B won't be a huge money-maker for you; but wait, you haven't gotten to your expenses yet. Get out the list of operating costs you drew up in Chapter 6 and using either actual figures or estimates, add up all of your expenses for the year. Include salaries, the mortgage and utilities, business loans, office expenses, food, linens, everything.

And don't forget about depreciation. Ask your accountant for advice on this, but chances are that you'll be able to deduct the amount that is deemed to depreciate on your house, office equipment, and other big-ticket items this year. This is not an out-of-pocket expense but will help lower your taxable profit, which will then lower your tax bill.

Don't forget about the interest you pay on any loans connected with the business. And remember that the type of business you run—sole proprietorship, partnership, or corporation—will also affect your profit and loss statement.

After deducting all of your expenses from your revenue, you'll be left with a pretax profit or loss. There's one more step, though. Now deduct all of the taxes you pay in connection with your business—except payroll taxes, which are figured into your payroll expenses—and you will come up with your actual net profit or loss, which probably seems a long way from your initial gross revenue figure.

Though you'll always have certain fixed expenses, there are a variety of ways you can adjust your profit and loss statement: reducing your expenses, raising your room rates, and increasing your marketing or the items you sell to guests, are just a few. Over time, you will be able to see which features at your B&B bring people back, and those that don't matter. Running a B&B is a constant experiment; your profit and loss statement is a constant reminder of how well your experiment is doing.

Improving Cash Flow

Even though your B&B will be a business where the cash flow will be highly erratic, you can to some extent predict when your cash flow will slow down and when it will be high. This will help you to see which months you should stockpile some of your excess cash in order to provide you with cash flow in the down times.

Cash flow is defined as the pattern of movement of cash in and out of a business: revenue and expenses. If you apply for a loan with a bank or other financial company after your business is up and running, you'll have to provide an analysis of your cash flow; if you're just starting out, you may be required to provide the loan officer with a projected cash flow statement.

Cash flow includes all actual monies coming in and going out of the business—cash, checks, and income from credit cards. Depreciation of your B&B home and other equipment does not factor into your cash flow analysis.

The first step to improving your cash flow is to increase your business year round. But the effects from this aren't always that immediate, and there are thing you can do to even out your cash flow a little more.

After analyzing your income projections, you might want to conduct special promotions designed to fill rooms during those times of the year when your cash flow most needs boosting. Here's an example that anticipates your guests' cash flow needs. In many areas, April is a slow month as well as tax time. You could offer a Tax Relief Cash Flow package, where you guarantee to improve your guests' cash flow with a deep discount. Special additional gimmicks might include a thermometer, a bottle of aspirin and a bottle of champagne for each couple who books two nights at your B&B between April 15th and May 15th, when business starts to pick up again.

Another way to even out your expenses and therefore improve your cash flow is to ask your utility companies to average out your payments so that you basically pay the same amount each month year round. And as I suggested earlier, if you stash away 20 percent of your gross revenue during the busy times, you'll have money to draw on during the slow months.

Keeping Track of Your Money

Most B&B owners use a variety of methods to help them keep track of their money, both revenue and expenses.

The basic record will probably be your checkbook. There are a number of business checking accounts that come with built-in ledgers where you can record your expenses under different expense categories at the same time you write a check. Separating these expenses in advance makes it easy at the end of the year to determine how much you've spent in each category, and if you need to cut back.

Some B&B hosts prefer to keep their financial records on computer. Software can keep track of your expenses and income, categorize them, add them up in a flash, and even print out checks. One-Write Plus by NEBS is one example.

To keep track of your revenue, you should keep a record of each reservation and guest visit: how many nights, room rate, taxes, and other expenses the guests incurred. There are a number of specialized B&B software programs that can help you keep track of your revenue and expenses, plus provide other features like word processing and database tracking. One such company is The InnManager, which will help you keep track of your finances and reservations. For more information, contact Jeff Koss at J.K. Software Systems, 28 Chapel Street, Portsmouth, New Hampshire 03801, or call 603-433-3252.

Whatever method you choose, make sure that it's easy to use and that you update it at least once a week. Going longer than that will make keeping track of your money a chore and something you're likely to put off; and you'll be more likely to make mistakes.

Fortunately, some of the companies that you'll do business with are making it easier for their customers to keep track of their money. Credit and charge card companies now offer a breakdown of charges in different categories on their monthly statement. Some of the suppliers with which you maintain an account will also provide this service. And if they don't already do this, ask. They might start.

Developing Your Credit

If you're in business for any length of time, you're going to need credit in one form or another. Most of the time, it will be from suppliers who deal with you on a regular basis and who don't deal in picking up cash or checks with each delivery. Not only is it too unwieldy and increases the possibility of loss, it's a big waste of time.

Most suppliers and other companies won't offer you credit unless you've done business with them before. It's the age-old Catch 22—how can you develop your credit if no one will give you any in the first place?

Fortunately, there are ways around this. Many companies will open a credit line for you based on your personal credit record. They'll usually start you out small and then increase your credit line as your history with them grows. Needless to say, you'll help your credit line if you always pay promptly, even before the due date—and by acting promptly whenever there is a question about your account.

With other suppliers, you'll need to prove yourself in the beginning, and your personal credit, no matter how stellar, will have nothing to do with it. These companies will make you pay cash or by check before they deliver the goods, and only after a certain period of time will they begin to extend you credit, and only a little at a time.

Once you begin to establish a credit record with your B&B, you'll undoubtedly be solicited by charge card companies that invite you to open a business account with a high credit limit and low monthly payments. Though having a business credit card account helps in many instances—such as renting a car or buying airline tickets in certain situations—try not to use them too much. Because cards are almost universally accepted—even the IRS takes MasterCard and Visa now—and it's easier to slap down the plastic than to apply for a basic account with a supplier, you might be tempted to run up huge bills with their inherent high interest charges. This is a high price to pay for apparent convenience. Instead, use them sparingly, appreciate them for what they are—an extremely expensive way to borrow money— and be as judicious with their use and payment as you are with your other creditors. After all, they can help develop your credit rating, too.

Although banks are a lot pickier now about lending money even to people with unblemished credit ratings, you might apply for a line of credit at your bank, if you don't have one already. Learning to rely on it only in emergency financial situations, then paying back the money as soon as possible will help your business get through the tough times, which you will certainly have.

Working With Suppliers

As I've already said, one part of working with suppliers is to build up credit and a working relationship. There are other ways as well.

Getting the best price may be the most important thing to you. Other B&B owners might be attracted by a company's twice-weekly delivery schedule, while still others might favor a supplier because of the particular brands the company carries.

Most suppliers will bend over backwards to get your business, though you may find that you'll have to jump through a few hoops at first, for instance, to get a credit account set up in your initial dealings with the company.

There are many ways to find the suppliers who will work with you and who you'll feel most comfortable working with. You should know if one supplier doesn't give you the terms you'd like, there are others who will. Don't sign on with one right away—take the time to shop around for the best price, the quality you want, and the working relationship you feel comfortable with. Whether you prefer to deal by mail and have the items delivered to your door or pick them up yourself, it's easy to find the best supplier for your B&B, from guest soaps stamped with your B&B's logo to business stationery to the chocolates you'll place on each guest's pillow.

Borrowing Money

The issue of borrowing money in these credit-weary days is apt to be a sticky one among B&B hosts who may have to take out a first or second mortgage to buy an existing B&B or start one from scratch. "I'm in enough debt already," you may say, "Why would I want to borrow any more?"

As you'll see in an upcoming section later in this chapter, sometimes your cash flow won't keep up with your expenses. Even if you or a partner holds down a steady job, trust me when I say there will be times when that won't be enough. Operating and maintaining a B&B with all of its expenses that continue steadily from month to month will eat up huge amounts of cash, and during those times, it may be necessary to borrow money.

If you have a rich relative or a sizable trust fund, you can skip over this section. But if you're like most of us, you'll need to rely on a conventional financing source.

I know of many examples where B&B hosts have drawn on their credit cards to initially finance their B&Bs, and then have gone back to them when the slow season hit. At anywhere from a 12 to 21 percent annual rate of interest, that's an expensive way to borrow money. Even if you fully intend to pay it back before interest has a chance to accumulate, there will be times when you are only able to make the minimum payment. And since you already know to anticipate these cycles, especially in a business that's usually known for its seasonal brand of tourism, you should take steps now to line up an available source of credit that you can draw upon immediately.

Some B&B owners form partnerships just for this reason: to have a silent partner with deep pockets who's looking for a good rate of return on his money. But if you prefer to have a partner for other reasons—or to go it alone—and you don't want to have to rely on your credit cards, there is another option, and that is to open a line of credit at your bank.

If you don't want to go this route—or get turned down—there is the old-fashioned way, and that is to save for a rainy day. When business is booming and revenue is strong, set aside a certain percentage—some say 20 percent of every room booked and paid for—and sock it away in an interest-bearing savings account. Don't invest it in a place where you don't have instant access to your funds—even though your interest rate may be better, you'll probably pay more by paying a penalty or fees for withdrawal from an IRA, mutual fund, or other investment. A money market fund is best; the interest rates tends to be a little higher than a passbook savings account, and you have immediate access to your money.

How to Raise Additional Capital

Because the revenue from a B&B can be sporadic at times, many B&B owners turn to other sources of income. Most other businesses are concerned with raising additional capital to initially finance their business—even though their cash flow may be cyclical, the ups and downs are probably not as extreme as the cash flow in a B&B. To raise additional capital to finance the B&B, some people turn to parents or relatives, while many rely on the proceeds from the sale of their primary house and move to start their B&B in an area where they can get a lot more house for their money. Indeed, this is the strategy of many people who decide to open a B&B as a retirement business, and they actually buy their B&B home outright. Unfortunately, enough of this may drive up real estate prices in the areas where they're moving. With a pension, Social Security, and other benefits intact and no mortgage to speak of, the monthly expenses required to run their B&B will be quite manageable from room revenue alone.

For others with mortgages and no regular income, the best way to raise the additional capital needed to keep the B&B afloat is to offer products connected with the B&B that you can sell to guests and non-guest visitors. In addition to the products described in Chapter 1, you could offer consulting or run seminars for aspiring B&B owners; self-publish a booklet of your favorite recipes from the B&B; sell mugs, T-shirts and caps imprinted with the logo of your B&B; or offer a guided tour and sightseeing service to tourists, who may then turn into paying guests.

You have to be creative to stay in business these days, no matter what your venture. The advantage of other products and services that you offer is that many of them will result in additional business for your B&B, thus bringing your efforts full-circle.

How to Give Credit to Customers

The primary way that most businesses extend credit to their customers is by accepting major credit cards. MasterCard, Visa, American Express, Discover, and Diner's Club are accepted by many B&Bs. The credit companies will charge a fee to set you up with their service, and then you'll pay the credit company a percentage of every transaction made by a customer, usually 2 percent to 5 percent. Your account is typically credited within one to three days after you entered the transactions into the system, and there are certain restrictions each company places on its members, depending on the amount your B&B will gross, among other factors. It is relatively simple to apply for privileges that will allow you to accept credit cards from your patrons.

However, some B&B hosts decide not to accept charge cards from their guests. Either their volume is too low to justify paying the commissions, or else the credit company places too many restrictions on them. Some have also said that the companies tend to have a patronizing attitude toward smaller companies—such as B&Bs—because they simply don't provide the commission revenue that larger businesses do.

Others just figure that if a guest wants to stay at their B&B, she'll come whether she pays for her stay with a credit card or a check. I've seen instances where people will decide not to eat at a particular restaurant because it doesn't accept credit cards—and no one in the party has enough cash—but not accepting credit cards tends not to be an issue when booking a stay at a B&B. However, there are good reasons to provide this service.

I also know of some B&B owners who, even though they do accept credit cards, will ask guests if they can instead pay by cash or check. Most guests agree without a fuss. In some cases, the B&B will give the guest a discount if they pay cash instead of using a credit card.

The most important reason for a B&B to accept credit cards concerns taking reservations over the phone. If a person calls in to make a reservation and has to back it up with a credit card number and a deposit that is instantly charged to their account, they're more likely to honor their reservation, even if the deposit is credited to a future stay should they cancel their reservation. Guests who call to make a reservation and are told that they can't be confirmed until they send in a check as a deposit, are more likely to not follow through, and you lose a booking. It's one more step to take in a world where people lean towards the easy way out because their world is getting more complicated by the day. They want to stay at your B&B to simplify it, and making it more complicated for them to come will just throw a wrench into the entire works.

So even if you hate the idea of credit cards, you should definitely arrange to accept them. It may be money in someone else's pocket if you don't.

Another way to arrange for certain customers to have credit is to set up a house charge account for regular patrons. If there are a number of local companies that book rooms with you frequently for guests or if you serve dinner to locals, they may make a request to open a house account to facilitate billing and also for the same reason that you may want to set up house accounts with other area businesses—so that you don't have to be fumbling with change and can build up a strong business relationship. This may also help them to impress their clients, which will then undoubtedly result in more business for you.

Any way you decide to extend credit to customers, it's important that you do offer it in some form. We have a love-hate relationship with it as a society, but since we do rely on it, you should arrange for it before you open your B&B.

Action Guidelines

✔ Calculate what your gross revenue would be with a 100 percent occupancy rate, as well as lesser amounts.

✔ Subtract your projected expenses from your estimated gross revenues to determine your profit or loss for the year.

✔ Work with your suppliers to develop a credit history based on your B&B and not your own personal credit rating.

✔ Select your financial source to help you through the slow seasons, whether it's a business partner or money that you've saved from peak times.

✔ Arrange with credit card companies to accept charge cards from your guests.

$$\widehat{} B\&B\ Profile \widehat{}$$

Michelle Sutor
Windmill Ranch
Albuquerque, New Mexico

Back in October of 1993, Michelle Sutor suddenly found herself the owner of a ranch that also doubled as a B&B, with a 7,200 square-foot main building to boot. And to think that she started out as a cook at the ranch.

Not that she didn't have experience, for Michelle had owned a bar and restaurant in New York City for five years when she decided that she'd had enough. She grew up in New Mexico, and decided to move back. In order to detox from the stress of being a restaurateur, she took a job as a cook at the Windmill Ranch. After Michelle had spent a year there, her boss decided to retire and move away. She offered the business to Michelle.

"At first I was in shock," she recalls. "And then, I started to think of different sidelines we could run here so that I could afford the ranch. I couldn't just do a B&B alone, especially when the mortgage was so high. But the property was so wonderful." So she decided to do it.

The B&B part of Windmill contains four guest rooms, all with queen-sized beds and private baths. The main house is a 95-year-old adobe home decorated in Southwestern style. Sutor was comfortable with the current B&B operations, so she turned her attentions to a six-car garage that was largely wasted space and converted it into a banquet facility accommodating 125 people. There's also an outdoor recreational facility as well as several places for wedding ceremonies and receptions.

Sometimes Michelle admits that all of the work of running these separate buildings makes them blur into one another after a while, but she says that it's necessary to keep them separate. "I've had to hire two secretaries to help me with bookkeeping since we took over here," she says. "To me, that is the most important thing, because if you mess up on the bookkeeping, then everything else will go downhill." She also hired a woman to take care of reservations while another does all of the computer work. Sutor also employs two ranch hands, and her husband works full-time doing landscaping and maintenance.

The Southwest and New Mexico both serve as big tourist attractions, and Michelle says that the beauty of the ranch is what attracts people. The Windmill is also right next to the Rio Grande. She markets the B&B by advertising in international publications and also paying for listings in B&B guidebooks. Occupancy at the Ranch ranges from 80 percent from October through December and drops down to 30 percent from January through March. Post-holiday times tend to be slow, but future plans for the winter off-season include operating a week-long health and fitness clinic at the ranch. Capacity will be limited to eight guests, and Sutor will hire a chef and a personal trainer.

She says that the biggest surprise to running a B&B, let alone a five-acre ranch, were the utility bills. Her favorite part of the business is meeting a lot of great people who visit from all over the world, and her least favorite part is having to get up at five in the morning.

The advice she has for aspiring B&B hosts is to make sure you know what you're getting into. "It also helps if you have some experience behind you, as well as being able to draw on a repertoire of special meals that you can cook for your guests," she adds. "But loving people is the most important thing. They do get on your nerves, so you do have to be a good actress."

GROWTH

G rowing a business today can be a challenge. Though everything you will do as the owner of your B&B will in some way influence how your business grows, most of the time your thoughts will not be on growth, but on putting out all of the little fires will pop up each day. If you have any time or energy left at the end of the day to think about growth, it may be along the lines of how to slow it down so that you'll have at least 15 minutes each day to call your own.

Seriously, growth—or the lack of it—is an issue that every B&B owner has to face at one time or another. This last chapter will show you how to deal with the variety of ways that growth will manifest itself in your B&B. And if you've gotten this far in your determination to open a B&B, handling growth will probably turn out to be the least of your troubles.

The Problems of Business Growth

Many B&B owners feel that of all the business problems to have, those that involve issues of growth are among the easiest to handle. It's not always so, however, Though growth as a rule means increased revenue and business, it also means more work and expenses, as well as more headaches.

Some B&Bs will grow at a slow steady rate of eight percent to 10 percent a year. Others will explode after a glowing article in a large-circulation magazine or newspaper appears. Which is better? While some prefer slow growth as a way to allow them to learn about the business and grow into it, others say that rapid or sudden growth provides them with a real education of what running a B&B is all about and a needed boost when the owner might have otherwise been hesitant about forging ahead. This kick in the pants is sometimes exactly what a B&B owner needs.

Growth *can* be managed and controlled to some extent. How you do it and whether you do it is up to you.

Some of the choice is manifested in the ability to choose your guests to some extent, although many B&B hosts would never think of doing this, equating the action of hanging out a No Vacancy sign at any time of year.

One issue you'll face with a growing B&B is whether or not to hire employees—or if you already have help, whether you should increase their hours to full-time or hire more workers.

Your B&B is your baby, and if you're used to doing it all yourself, you may find it hard to delegate some of the responsibility to someone else, even if it means more free time for you. Most B&B owners have difficulty letting go at first, but with time and as you begin to see the ability of the people you do hire, you will trust in them more, which will leave you with time to address problems in the business.

Another byproduct of growth is what to do with the extra money. Some B&B hosts use it to pay off some of their personal debts, but the IRS will count these monies as personal income. It's best to repay debt over time, though some people feel that the savings you'll make in not paying debt interest will more than offset the increased tax you'll have to pay.

Some B&B hosts use the extra money to pay off business debts, such as the mortgage. Though it may feel good to own your own house free and clear, the deductible interest portion of your monthly mortgage payment can come in handy in keeping your taxes down, especially since your business will likely show a larger profit with increased income.

One method that many B&B owners use to invest the money and keep their profits and therefore their taxes down is to embark on a sizable capital improvement project once a year. For instance, during the slow travel months of March or April, many B&Bs will close their doors and add private baths to a couple of guest rooms, remodel the dining room, redecorate some of the guest rooms, or add a deck or swimming pool. This, will enhance the desirability and value of their B&B, and they'll be able to charge more for the rooms. The extra cash will provide them with more money for next year's off-season projects. Of course, as I explained in Chapter 6, you will have to show a profit three out of five years if you're operating as a sole proprietorship or partnership. But if you've been growing steadily, this will not be a problem.

How to Solve Business Problems

Every day that you're running your B&B, you will run into problems. Some, like running out of bread or not having a room made up for guests who arrive early, will be easy to remedy. For others, like how to treat your first travel writer or what to do when the furnace breaks down or the pipes freeze on Christmas Eve and you're booked solid, you'll need help, whether in the form of paid services or good advice from other B&B owners who have been through it all already.

With some problems, whether they're major or minor, you'll be so busy that you won't have time to think about your options. You'll dig right in then and there and do whatever it takes to get the job done.

Building up a good relationship with other B&B owners in your area will provide you a network of experienced people who can give you advice. In turn, they will turn to you at some point in the future for your advice and help, as well.

Your fellow B&B hosts won't be able to answer all of your questions or provide solutions to every problem, however. For that, your local or regional chamber of commerce and tourist boards may help, at least in terms of more specific marketing advice or broad advice, like the types of visitors who've come to the area in the last year based on their marketing survey.

In fact, you'll find a ready number of people who you already deal with who are able to work with you to help you solve the problems unique to your business. Your accountant can also help you determine how one capital improvement to your B&B and the projected income it will bring will affect the taxes you'll have to pay next year. And for another perspective, a B&B host a few towns over can tell you how her business changed because she made the same kind of renovation that you're currently considering.

The representative you work with at your bank can also help you with your business problems, as well as your lawyer, your real estate agent, and other business owners in your town. In fact, just when you think that there's no one you can turn to for help for your business, you'll discover a surfeit of people ready and willing to help you—and most of the time, the advice will be free.

No matter what kind of brick wall you'll come up against in running your B&B, you will be able to find help.

Managing Employees for Efficiency

The art of management once prescribed that the boss or manager rule with an iron grip in one hand and a whip in the other. Just like any strict disciplinarian parents and children, both employer and employee were clear on who was in charge. The employee went along with this facade but more often than not managed to get away with things whenever possible and did only what was expected and never anything more.

The opposite philosophy was that of the sensitive manager. He soft-pedaled harsh news, coddled his employees, and always was ready to heap lavish praise at the tiniest accomplishment. Again, employees went along with it, but felt they were never fully trusted or appreciated for their own talents and efforts. As before, quality and morale suffered.

The ideal management style for a small business is to let employees feel as though they are responsible for the business's success or failure; that is, they treat the business as though it were their own, and also accept certain responsibilities.

This style is perfect for B&B owners who need to delegate, and also because B&B employees tend to very quickly develop a personal relationship with the boss. The type of management that's required may run counter to what many people think being a boss ought to be; but in the end, you'll find that your employees will be happier, more productive, and will stay with you longer if you learn to manage them in this way.

It's not easy to do this, however. People who feel they have to control their employees in order to get them to work may run into problems with executing this altered style of management. However, once you see that your employees will treat your business almost as well as you do, it won't take long for you to become a proponent of this management style and actually begin to adopt it in other areas of your life.

Here's how to do it. Say you need to hire an employee to work 20 hours a week at your B&B, helping out wherever you happen to need it. First, determine the tasks she says she's best at, and which of those she would feel comfortable being left alone to execute.

Train her by going through the various tasks she'll need to become familiar with, from answering the phone to cleaning a room to checking in a guest. Have her watch you do it a few times, and then let her go off to do it herself. Assure her that she can approach you with any questions she has, no matter how trivial they may seem to her. Encourage her to maintain open communication with you at all times. Your end of the deal is to remain open to her queries and always respond in a patient manner.

Then, once it appears she has one task down pat, send another her way. For instance, if she's comfortable with taking reservations, you might let her take the next logical step, sending out confirmation letters with your brochure and perhaps a handwritten note, if she isn't doing that already. Then when the guests that she booked arrive, watch the interaction and your employee's happiness.

If she makes mistakes, call them to her attention immediately, and then patiently and without judgment, explain to her the way to do it that's best for the B&B and *why*. Make sure that it's not just because she's doing the tasks a bit differently from how you would. In fact, for maximum efficiency, try not to get too caught up with how things get done, rather, make sure that they do get done. If you insist that your employees follow certain steps in order to reach the final solution, you'll find that you'll be trying to squeeze a lot of round pegs into square holes. The outcome may be the same, but the morale will drop, as will your efficiency.

Then, as your employee's responsibilities grow, increase her pay based on performance and give regular bonuses and days off with pay. The idea is for her to feel personally responsible for your—and her—guests' happiness so that you're free to work on other projects without worrying about the business.

The secret to successfully managing employees is to show them what to do, trust that they'll do it, and then leave them alone. Though many employees will be taken aback by this unique approach, and some will find it to be too alien for their tastes, the great majority will meet the challenge and help build your business while cultivating a personal relationship with you and your guests.

Some B&B owners are perfectionists, however, and they think that no one but themselves knows how to do things the right way. Unfortunately, this kind of manager will find it hard to keep employees, and may be burned out by the end of the first year in the business. Though you're still calling the shots, compromise and acceptance is the name of the game when it comes to managing employees and maintaining the steady growth of your B&B.

Business Alliances

As already suggested, it's a great idea to join the local chamber of commerce, tourism board, or B&B association so that you can meet your colleagues in the hospitality field. In far too many cases, business owners will look upon other businesses as competition—even if they're in an unrelated field.

But joining forces with other businesses—B&Bs and others—can more than double their marketing efforts and scope, resulting in increased business for all concerned. If you join the local chamber of commerce or tourist board, you can meet other people whose aims are the same as yours: to get guests to stay overnight at their B&B. With others in different businesses—like an antique store, local tour guide, or even a candy shop—you can band together and offer package deals. And because you're both marketing the package, not only do you reach different groups of people, but you'll also reach some of the same people twice. And study after study has shown that people rarely respond the first time they read an ad or brochure. If a potential customer hears about your package twice in two different venues, she'll be more likely to inquire about the package or at least remember it for the future.

But the most valuable part of forming alliances with other businesses is the feedback, ideas and advice from other business owners who may run their businesses in a totally different way than you do. At first, your reaction may be to scoff at ideas that vary so much from yours. But keep an open mind as you listen to what worked and what didn't. As you listen, think about how you could apply the same techniques to your own business or alter them to fit the idiosyncrasies of your B&B. Even if you paid a consultant big bucks for ideas on how to run your business better, they're still only the ideas of one person—better to consider many ideas before discarding some than to rely too heavily on one and then fail.

Perhaps the best example of a business alliance in the B&B business is to form an association of other B&B owners in your area if one doesn't exist already. The benefits for most organizations formed this way are twofold: first, you have an instant group of peers who are familiar with what you're doing, and can tell you about their own experiences. Second, joining forces allows you to market each business more effectively because it's also being marketed as part of an associated entity. For instance, most B&B associations combine forces because they're in the same town or state or because they share a common theme—farm B&B, romantic B&B, or city B&B. They'll assemble a brochure that lists the name of the association on the cover and describes all of the member B&Bs inside and how they differ from each other; i.e., whether they accept children or smokers, their price range. Members then distribute the brochure through the normal channels of the chamber of commerce, tourist board, and by mail to people who read about the group in ads and editorial mentions. One of the members typically serves as the main contact for the group, and may refer callers to the B&B that's most appropriate to their needs. Other B&B associations get a separate telephone number and then rotate it each day or week among the members.

Again, not only can the association serve as a coalition that combines the marketing strengths of all the members—after all, individual B&B owners will market their B&Bs in slightly different ways from other members—but if a tourist picks up your B&B's brochure, then sees your name listed in the B&B association brochure, that's another exposure for you and another chance at increased recognition and bookings.

Your business alliance or association doesn't necessarily have to be with other B&Bs, however. Hooking up with other businesses whose aims are similar to yours is bound to help everyone's bottom line.

Secret of Success

In my opinion, along with many B&B owners nationwide, the number one key to success in the industry is marketing. In this instance, I use the term quite broadly: not only encompassing all of the traditional channels, like advertising and publicity, but also your public relations campaign and how you interact with your guests.

During every minute that a guest spends at your B&B, you should be marketing yourself and the stay. I'm not talking about the hard sell; after all, you've already got them there. The secret of success is to get them to return, and to tell their friends about the wonderful experience they had at your B&B. This means being constantly aware of their happiness and comfort and recognizing opportunities to enhance their stay. Some guests won't welcome this degree of personal interaction with you; therefore, you'll have to let the ambiance of your B&B do your marketing for you.

It's impossible to predict in advance from a brief phone conversation what kind of interaction a guest welcomes. But in the day-to-day operations of running a B&B, you'll learn a lot about people in a very short period of time. Some characteristics you won't like or necessarily approve of, but it's all part of owning a B&B.

But remember, your marketing job never ends, and that goes for both kinds: through the media and also while your guests are staying with you. If you cease to market it either way, you will soon fade from their memory. After all, with thousands of messages bombarding customers each day, you need to stand out to succeed. But that doesn't mean a constant hard sell, either.

So whether a guest marvels at your brochure enough to make a reservation, oohs and aahs over the architectural detail in your B&B, or—most importantly—leaves your B&B thinking of you as family, and already looking forward to their next stay with you, you must always be marketing.

That and your happiness in running the B&B are the keys to success if you do decide to open a B&B.

Four Typical Problems and Solutions

Though each business will face its own unique set of problems depending on whether you start the business from scratch or buy an operating B&B, your location, the style of your B&B, and whether you're open year-round or just seasonally, there are some problems that most B&B owners will face at one time or another. Here are some of the most common, along with solutions.

I had a horrible experience with a guest who was hostile and abusive. I tried to calm her down, but her actions upset other guests, and so far none of the guests who were here that night have come back. What should I do in the future to deal with such a guest?

A: Ask her to leave. Many B&B owners find that guests who are pleasant and accommodating when sober turn into absolute monsters after they've had a few drinks or after an incident where they believe they've been slighted in some way. And there're a handful of guests who have discovered that if they make a scene and complain about everything in sight, the B&B owner will comp their room rate and meals.

This is the wrong way to handle it, because these few will just go on to the next B&B and do the same thing. No matter what the cause is, you must ask an abusive guest to leave at once and refund her money on the spot before it gets too much out of hand. This is necessary to preserve your reputation and relationship with the other guests who are witnessing the scene. Keep in mind they're probably on your side and embarrassed for you.

If the guest refuses to leave, call the police. This alone may cause her to leave. Try not to let it bother you when she hurls insults your way or threatens to sue. With no previous complaints on record, the officer, who's probably a fellow resident of the town, will probably escort the unruly guest out and throw you a sympathetic look.

I know I should put money away to help pay the bills when business slows down, but there are always so many other bills that demand my attention that I never seem to get around to it. Also, I'm working so hard when we're full that I feel I deserve a reward. Help!

A: Consider putting money aside for your rainy days the same way you pay your bills. Decide in advance the percentage of your gross deposits that you're going to put into savings, and then do it automatically when you go to the bank.

Ten or twenty percent may not seem like a lot, but it does add up. And keep in mind that the reason why a number of B&Bs fail is because they don't have enough cash to make it through the downtimes. You may decide to take a job in the interim, but that will definitely interfere with your ability to attract a full house for the following season, that is, if you intend to run the B&B as a full-time business. So keep stashing it away.

As for rewards, the best kind of treat any B&B host can give herself is some spare time, which doesn't cost anything. So whether you go out for an afternoon, or take yourself to the movies, consider this to be the best reward you could give yourself. But you probably already know this.

My B&B keeps me extremely busy but by the end of the day I look back and I don't seem to have accomplished much. The problem is that the phone rings whenever I'm in the middle of something, or a guest asks me a question and we end up talking for a half hour, or one of a million other interruptions comes up. What can I do?

A: Learn to make lists, delegate, and take advantage of the quiet times that do occur in the course of each day. Some chronic list-makers, however, regularly put more on their list than they could ever hope to accomplish in a week, let alone a day. If you fall into this category, start by chopping your list in half, or even by three-fourths. That way, if you check off everything on your list and there's still a few hours in the day, you can always add a few more.

Most work at a B&B gets done in short spurts in between a variety of interruptions, though most owners would prefer to have quiet, uninterrupted periods of time in which to work. Your task is to make an effort to schedule more uninterrupted periods during the day in order to allow you to concentrate on your work.

The best way to do this is to let someone else play front man for you. Hire someone for an afternoon or two each week to answer the phone and deal with guests and salespeople who might drop in. Your instructions should include that you are not to be interrupted for any reason. Then go somewhere so you can be sure you won't. Retreat to a far corner of the house, seek refuge in a friend's B&B, or even go to the library.

If this is impossible, or if you find you need even more time, you might want to take advantage of the time of the day when there will be the least amount of demands on your time. If you're not ready to sleep, late night can be a marvelously quiet time when you can accomplish office or other work. Early mornings usually don't work, since your attention will be on preparing breakfast, and some guests who are early birds may be up long before you are.

The trick is to find what works best for you and then stick to it, because it will always be extremely easy to let the day slide into night working 12 or more hours a day, but with the feeling that you got absolutely nothing done.

I'm opening my B&B in a month, and I have nothing with which to decorate it besides the furniture, quilts, and linens left by the previous owner. Without knickknacks and pictures, the place looks empty.

A: This is an easy one. Head for the yard sales, thrift shops and junk stores for china, doilies, pictures, and pottery that will add some character to your B&B. One B&B owner told me that she had inherited an entire stock of old plates from the previous owner, and she really didn't like them, but was determined to leave them in place until she was able to buy new ones. In the meantime, another B&B owner in town told her she should tell guests who asked about the trinkets and china that it all belonged to her great-grandmother, since that's what guests at B&Bs in the country expect.

Well, she balked at this and decided to be patient and learn to live with the offensive items. And her guests didn't really care one way or another. But another way to get quality art and decorations for free is to contact local artists and craftspeople and tell them they can display their work in the common areas of your B&B and offer them for sale. They should place a small label in a lower corner of the painting or on the bottom of the piece of pottery, and make up a few calligraphied cards and place them on tables informing guests that the artwork is for sale. Then split the sale price with the artist. You might even call your B&B a gallery and market it as such. This will not only increase your revenues but also help bring prospective guests to your B&B.

Reality Check

All B&B owners experience a time when they're so busy, or so involved with business, that they tune out the world as a whole and don't venture beyond the house except to go grocery shopping. Some even get someone else to perform these outside tasks for them.

If you're beginning to get the idea that a B&B is the perfect business for the most extreme brand of homebody, you're right. And it might seem that way on the surface. But in time, anyone who creates a tiny, self-contained world that admits in people from the outside but rarely allows the ringleader out, well, this loss of perspective will begin to harm the business. Even with regular contact with lots of people, if you don't venture out at least a few times a week, it's entirely possible that your attitude will begin to scare off guests.

When you open a B&B, you'll be operating your business from and in your home. If you're used to commuting to an office every day, you should be prepared for a shock. You'll have to motivate yourself, and there will be no one else around to do it. In addition, the constant interruptions, lack of personal time, and having strangers sleep in your home most nights of the week can quickly begin to skew your perspective on life and the world.

That's why it's imperative to get away from the business for a full afternoon or evening at least once a week. Do something that has nothing to do with the business, and don't use it as an excuse to get together with other B&B owners you know.

Do something for yourself for an extended period of time. After all, you'll be doing for other people for most of your waking hours. Take some time for yourself to insure that there will be some of you left over to give. Or else, you'll need to refer to the next section a little sooner than necessary.

When to Quit

Burnout is the number one reason why B&B owners decide to sell or close down their businesses. It's so very easy to become caught up in your business—after all, you are actually giving a performance to your guests, and all that attention and praise can be very gratifying to the ego. Which is precisely why many B&B owners keep doing more and more of it—and why a few don't want to share any with staff members.

The second reason why B&B owners decide to get out of the business is closely related to reason number one: running a successful B&B—or an unsuccessful one, for that matter, is a lot more difficult than it appears on the surface. They underestimate the amount of work and overestimate the money that the B&B will generate—especially the money they think will be available for their personal use.

Because of these skewed expectations, people tend to quit the business long before they originally planned. Five to seven years is frequently cited as the typical amount of time a B&B owner will be in business before getting the feeling it's time to move on to something else. However, I have heard of people who decide to leave after owning a B&B for only a year.

You'll know it's time to quit when:

- You no longer become excited about meeting a new guest.
- You can't remember the last vacation you took where you didn't stay at a B&B.
- You decide not to do your annual spring remodeling project.
- You can't remember the last time you woke up feeling refreshed.
- You're so burned-out you've lost your enthusiasm for most things.

Of course, B&B owners who still love the business may feel one or all of these symptoms at one time or another. The reason one may decide not to do the annual remodeling project is so she can spend two weeks in Jamaica doing absolutely nothing, because if she doesn't get a break, she won't have the desire to keep running the business.

The secret to knowing when to quit is when you feel like moving on and believe the disadvantages of running a B&B outweigh the advantages.

You may decide to opt out of the business, and in fact, may sell your business to a new B&B host. ("Remember when we were that enthusiastic?" you might say.) But many B&B owners who leave the business jump right back in a few years later. Typical excuses may include: "We didn't know how to live in a quiet house" or "We missed having the world come to stay with us."

So take heed—once you start, you may not be able to stop. After all, B&B gets in your blood.

Action Guidelines

✔ Be prepared to not like every aspect of growth.

✔ Build a network of supportive colleagues and business professionals you can rely on when you need to.

✔ Learn to manage employees with a hands-off attitude.

✔ Work with other B&Bs to increase business for all of you.

✔ Keep in mind that marketing your B&B is a non-stop venture.

✔ Keep your perspective on your life by taking regular breaks from the business.

⬯ *B&B Profile* ⬯

Jackie Jacquin
St. Mary's Glacier B&B
Idaho Springs, Colorado

Jackie Jacquin and her husband, Steve, cut their teeth in the B&B business by first running a one-room homestay for four years, which consisted of one room with a private bath. "We could accommodate one couple every weekend," she said, and that sufficed for a while.

Steve actually started the homestay, and Jackie helped him after they met, and they both enjoyed the work very much. "The problem was that we were turning a lot of people away," said Jackie. The solution was to close down the room and expand to a five-room B&B, all with private baths.

They expanded their business from 1,100 square feet up to almost 7,000 square feet. Although they both expected the construction and the B&B to be a lot of work, neither one realized the extent of the work, as well as being tied down to the house. "We pretty much need to be here all the time," said Jackie. But they have a unique way of taking turns running the B&B, getting out into the world, and bringing in some extra income.

Steve and Jackie share a teaching job in an elementary school in Denver, which is about an hour's drive from Idaho Springs. On alternate days, Jackie will make the trip and teach math, then Steve will go in and teach science.

Despite their schedule, the Jacquins do spend a lot of time together, and say that other couples who are considering opening a B&B as a joint business realize this. "You have to enjoy spending time together, and it's a good idea if you complement each other in the different parts of running the business," she adds.

One way that she's seen couples torn apart by the business is that they don't realize the amount of time and energy a B&B

requires. "Especially in your first year, you're working all the time, but it's very rewarding because you meet the neatest people, and a lot of these people return again and again," she says. Because they had experience running the one-room homestay, Jackie says that her impressions of a B&B were realistic, though she admits that the homestay was more of a hobby than a business. "At the time, we were both teaching full-time, and if we wanted to close it for the weekend, we could because it wasn't how we made our living," she says. Now, things are a little different.

She tries to spend two hours a day on marketing the B&B, and says that finding time for it is her biggest problem. "You have to make time to do the marketing," she says. "I could get all caught up in cleaning and cooking, but I can't do that unless I get people up here. A unique initiative of ours is that we actively work to attract corporate seminar and retreat business. We make contact with different businesses by sending out invitations to the person who plans retreats for their company, so they can visit our place and see if it's right for the company. We try to get our name out there as much as possible. Even if someone gets the brochure and it sits on the refrigerator behind a magnet, at least it's there," she adds.

When they first opened the B&B in August 1993, the Jacquins hired a marketing person to help them plan their strategy. Today, he holds workshops where he gives the Jacquin's name to potential corporate customers and vice versa. "On one retreat here," says Jackie, "a company in Denver brought in eight regional managers from all over the country and we put them up and gave them breakfast, lunch, and dinner for three days." They will also go through the phone book and call a company that seems to be the type that is looking for an out-of-the-way place to have a meeting. Today, a lot of businesses—and pleasure travelers—are looking for something different than the Holiday Inn conference experience, which only helps anyone who chooses to open a B&B.

Appendix
A

SAMPLE BUSINESS PLAN

This business plan is for a B&B that a young professional couple is thinking of buying in a nearby town.

The Berry Patch Bed & Breakfast

Blueberry Hill
Canterberry, New Hampshire 03333

603-555-6543

A Business Plan by Carol and Richard Jamm

STATEMENT OF PURPOSE

This business plan will serve as an operational guide and general policy manual for The Berry Patch Bed & Breakfast.

Carol and Richard Jamm are looking to borrow $150,000 for the purpose of purchasing and reopening The Berry Patch Bed & Breakfast, in Canterberry, New Hampshire. Most of the funds, $125,000, will go toward the purchase of the physical building and 2.5 acres of land. The house will serve as collateral for the mortgage. The remaining $25,000 will be in the form of a line of credit. This will be used toward upgrading the furnace, replacing linens and dishes, and for initial marketing costs. The principals are also investing $50,000 of their own money for operating expenses, working capital, and a cash reserve fund.

TABLE OF CONTENTS

SECTION ONE: THE BUSINESS

A. Description of Business

The Berry Patch Bed & Breakfast is a rural five-bedroom bed-and-breakfast inn that caters to urban visitors, primarily from the Boston area. Room rates range from $85 to $125 a night. At the present time, annual occupancy rate is 60 percent.

The Nutts, the current owners, started the B&B in May 1985. The B&B is open year-round and serves breakfast to overnight guests only.

The Berry Patch Bed & Breakfast is located in a high-traffic tourist area, which means the occupancy rate is actually close to 100 percent during July and August. It drops after Labor Day but is booked solid on weekends in the spring and fall.

Occupancy can be increased with special promotions and discounts during the off-season. Carol Jamm is a former marketing executive at Hilton Hotels, Inc., and is familiar with the kinds of marketing strategies that will attract guests to The Berry Patch Bed & Breakfast. She also will actively pursue local corporations that need a small, private building for conferences and executive retreats.

B. Description of the Market

The Berry Patch Bed & Breakfast will continue to provide restful nights in comfortable, antique-filled rooms to guests, along with a gourmet breakfast the next morning. The plan is to increase the occupancy rate from 60 percent to 80 percent over the course of 18 months.

The goal of The Berry Patch Bed & Breakfast is to become a B&B known for personalized service to guests, as well as attention to detail. The target market is young, unmarried couples in the Boston area, which is two hours south of The Berry Patch Bed & Breakfast.

The owners will pursue this desirable market through the following:

- Publicity in newspapers in Boston and throughout New England
- Advertising in Boston and New England lifestyle magazines
- Direct mail promotions to the B&B's existing house list
- Guest referral discounts on future stays

The owners will pursue the corporate market through the following:

- Make cold calls to travel planners at local and Boston corporations
- Invite qualified prospects for a free overnight stay
- Publicize and advertise the program in local and regional business publications

C. Description of Location

The Berry Patch Bed & Breakfast is located two miles outside of the village of Canterberry, on a quiet road with little traffic. This will appeal to guests who are looking or a quiet place to stay. Canterberry attracts many visitors to the Shaker Village, which is the major tourist attraction in town. Concord, the state capitol, and the Lakes Region are a short drive away.

The house is a 13-room Cape built in 1803 with several additions made over the years. The guest rooms are quaint yet functional; the downstairs common areas are large and provide a quiet haven for guests. There is a broad expanse of lawn out back with a pond for swimming and ice skating. The land abuts a protected nature preserve where guests can wander on the hiking trails.

The owner's quarters consist of a two-bedroom apartment located in an ell off the back of the house.

2

D. Description of the Competition

There are two inns and one other B&B in Canterberry that will be competing directly with The Berry Patch Bed & Breakfast.

The Lincoln Bed & Breakfast is a three-room facility located in the village of Canterberry. The rooms are not as luxurious as those at The Berry Patch Bed & Breakfast and are priced at $50 a night per couple. The owner is a schoolteacher who runs the B&B as a sideline business. The B&B is only open from May through October. She's been running the business for eight years and apparently has no plans to expand, since she has kept the B&B pretty much the same since she opened it.

The Shaker Inn is a 20-room inn located in an historic building. This inn also operates a full restaurant serving breakfast, lunch, and dinner to the public as well as to guests.

A big part of the Inn's business focuses on weddings, banquets, and other private functions. Even though they have a large number of guest rooms, it almost seems as though the lodging business is operated as an afterthought.

Tourists who are not looking for the kind of intimacy that The Berry Patch Bed & Breakfast provides will prefer to stay at the Shaker Inn. However, due to lack of promotion, they may not know it exists.

The Inn has also experienced a change in management four times in five years, with new owners coming in twice during that period. We feel that this lack of stability contributes to the problems the Inn has had with both its identity and its occupancy rate.

The Lake House Bed & Breakfast is a four-room B&B that comes closest to what is envisioned for The Berry Patch Bed & Breakfast. The owners have operated the B&B for three years and do a lot of promotion and community-oriented events.

The Lake House Bed & Breakfast is elegant but not so sophisticated that it will scare some guests away. The B&B's

3

weak spot, however, is service, which we plan to stress at The Berry Patch Bed & Breakfast. Both of the principal owners at The Lake House work—one at an outside job, the other at a quilting business at home—and it seems that their attention is a bit scattered, because the B&B can be immaculate inside (we looked), but they can go a week without mowing the lawn. People notice things like that.

There are other inns and B&Bs in outlying towns along Route 112, but none offers the rural location of The Berry Patch Bed & Breakfast.

E. Description of Management

Carol Jamm served as marketing manager for Hilton Hotels from 1987 through 1992, when she moved to New Hampshire with her husband specifically to look for a bed-and-breakfast to purchase and operate. She received an MBA in marketing from Boston University. Her first jobs were with the Hilton corporation, in the marketing departments at individual hotels in the chain.

Richard Jamm operated his own small construction business after graduating from high school. The size of his workforce has varied over the years, but he has managed at least five full-time employees at any one time.

Carol will be in charge of marketing and managing the office while Richard will handle the day-to-day operations as well as maintaining and making improvements to the physical plant.

The Jamms have retained the services of both an attorney and an accountant to help set up the business. They intend to join the local chamber of commerce, regional bed-and-breakfast association, and the tourism board in order to provide feedback and network with colleagues.

4

F. Description of Personnel

In the beginning, The Berry Patch Bed & Breakfast will hire one part-time employee to assist with serving breakfast, making up rooms, and general office work. Pay will be $5.50 an hour to start, with no benefits. We anticipate this job to consist of 20 hours a week. In slow times, this position will either be cut down or eliminated depending on our slow season.

We don't anticipate the need for additional employees in the near future.

G. Application and Expected Effect of Loan or Investment

We will also invest $50,000 of our own money into the property, resulting in a total of $200,000.

The $150,000 will be used as follows:

Purchase of Blueberry Hill property	$125,000
Renovations	25,000
Working capital	15,000
Cash reserve	10,000
Total:	$ 175,000

The Nutts, the current owners, are burnedout and eager to sell, which helped to result in this favorable deal. Before any renovations, an independent appraisal company assessed the property at $175,000.

Early renovations that we plan for the business include shoring up and reinforcing the sagging front porch, painting the exterior of the house, doing new landscaping, and generally sprucing up the guest rooms and common areas where it's especially needed.

5

The amount of working capital will allow The Berry Patch Bed & Breakfast to pay the associated costs of transferring an existing business, joining trade associations, subscribing to industry newsletters, refurbishing inventory, meeting initial expenses, and building up a reserve fund for the off-season, when expenses remain constant but revenue dips drastically.

We've arranged with the Canterberry Bank for a special reserve line of credit to be used in case of major repairs to the house, or other emergencies. We will be investing $50,000 of our own funds toward the B&B.

H. Summary

The Berry Patch Bed & Breakfast is an elegant, low-key B&B where the emphasis is on service. Carol and Richard Jamm, the prospective owners of The Berry Patch Bed & Breakfast, are seeking $200,000 to turn the B&B into what their vision of the ideal bed-and-breakfast should be. The money will enable them to set up the business, renovate and repair the property before reopening the business, have a line of credit in reserve along with adequate working capital in order to do the business right. This amount will allow the Jamms to bring the B&B through the transition from one owner to another, and to take the time necessary to convert the B&B into a showplace.

There will always be a demand for lodging facilities in the Canterberry area. Even without doing any marketing, the previous owners were able to maintain a 60 percent occupancy rate. The combination of Carol's marketing savvy and Richard's entrepreneurial skills will ensure the increased and continued success of The Berry Patch Bed & Breakfast.

6

SECTION TWO: FINANCIAL DATA

A. Sources and Applications of Funding

The Berry Patch Bed & Breakfast

Sources:
1. Mortgage loan	$125,000
2. Line of credit	25,000
3. New investment from Jamms	50,000
Total:	$200,000

Applications:
1. Purchase Blueberry Hill property	$125,000
2. Renovations	25,000
3. Working capital	15,000
4. Cash reserve for contingencies	10,000

To be secured by the assets of the business and personal guarantees of the principals, Carol and Richard Jamm

7

B. Income Projections by Month, Year One

	Jan	Feb	Mar	Apr	May	Jun	Jul	Aug	Sep	Oct	Nov	Dec	Total
Cash Receipts	$2,100	$3,200	$2,500	$1,575	$1,800	$3,000	$4,200	$4,200	$3,700	$4,000	$1,700	$2,500	$34,475
Total Cash Receipts	$2,100	$3,200	$2,500	$1,575	$1,800	$3,000	$4,200	$4,200	$3,700	$4,000	$1,700	$2,500	$34,475
Cash Disbursements													
Mortgage	$775	$775	$775	$775	$775	$775	$775	$775	$775	$775	$775	$775	9300
Insurance	$100	$100	$100	$100	$100	$100	$100	$100	$100	$100	$100	$100	1200
Utilities	300	350	275	250	200	200	200	200	225	325	350	350	3225
Office Supplies	25	25	25	25	25	25	25	25	25	25	25	25	300
Telephone	115	115	115	115	115	115	115	115	115	115	115	115	1380
Credit card commisions	81	90	85	50	60	105	145	145	125	135	55	85	1161
Postage	50	50	50	50	50	50	50	50	50	50	50	50	600
Marketing & Advertising	125	125	125	125	125	125	125	125	125	125	125	125	1500
Legal & accounting fees	100	100	100	100	100	100	100	100	100	100	100	100	1200
Food	125	200	150	100	100	180	240	240	200	220	75	125	1955
Guest Toiletries	55	55	55	55	55	55	55	55	55	55	55	55	660
Miscellaneous	40	40	40	40	40	40	40	40	40	40	40	40	480
Total Cash Disbursements	1891	2025	1895	1785	1745	1870	1970	1970	1935	2065	1865	1945	22961
Net Cash Flow	$209	$1,175	$605	($210)	$55	$1,125	$2,230	$2,230	$1,765	$1,935	($165)	$555	$11,509
Cumulative Cash Flow	$209	$1,384	$1,989	$1,779	$1,834	2959	$5,189	$7,419	$9,184	$11,119	$10,954	$11,509	
Cash on Hand													
Opening Balance	$2,500	$2,709	$3,884	$4,489	$4,279	$4,334	$5,464	$7,434	$9,664	$11,429	$13,364	$13,199	
Plus Cash Receipts	$2,100	$3,200	$2,500	$1,575	$1,800	$3,000	$4,200	$4,200	$3,700	$4,000	$1,700	$2,500	
Minus Cash Disbursements	$1,891	$2,025	$1,895	$1,785	$1,745	$1,870	$2,230	$1,970	$1,935	$2,065	$1,865	$1,945	
Total=New Balance	$2,709	$3,884	$4,489	$4,279	$4,334	$5,464	$7,434	$9,664	$11,429	$13,364	$13,199	$13,754	

8

SAMPLE MARKETING PLAN

I consider drawing up a marketing plan to be barely secondary to writing your business plan. Your business plan will serve as your anchor; a marketing plan will be your rudder. Again, it's important to take the time now to discover all of your marketing options, and then choose the ones that will work best for you.

Refer to the following plan when planning the marketing strategies for your business.

Sample Marketing Plan

Mary, the owner of The Dew Drop Inn, has been running the business for two years. Most of her marketing budget has gone for advertising in regional magazines and ads in the weekly newspaper, and the annual guide the local tourism association publishes. Mary is unhappy with the results. Drawing up an annual marketing plan allowed her to revamp her strategy and anticipate certain times of the year that would require more time and money.

Her allotted budget of $3,000 for the year—5 percent of gross revenue of $60,000—comes out to $250 a month. But the months that require more planning, and therefore more expenditures, are reflected in the chart.

Keep in mind that this is how one business does it. Use this format, but tailor your own marketing expectations and budget to the timetable.

1995 MARKETING PLAN FOR THE DEW DROP INN

Goals:

- To decrease reliance on advertising and create promotions that attract attention.
- To spread out marketing tasks between my full-time office assistant, Denise, and myself.
- To spend 10 hours a week on marketing.
- To bring in more families from the Boston area.

Month	Media	Execution	Budget
January	Direct Marketing: Send March discount weekend coupons to house list	Denise	400 past guests & 600 prospective guests Postage: 1,000 x .29 = $290 Stationery: $150 Printing coupon: $60 Total: $500
	Advertising: One weekly newspaper ad	Mary	4 x $30/per ad = $120
	Publicity: Send press release to local papers and magazines about March discount program	Denise	Postage: $10

Month	*Media*	*Execution*	*Budget*
February (busy month)	Direct Marketing: Send brochures to prospective customers who call.	Mary	120 x .29 = $34.80
	Advertising: One weekly newspaper ad	Mary	4 x $30 = $120
	Publicity: None		
March	Direct Marketing: None		
	Advertising: Magazines send letters exhorting her to advertise in summer issues.	Mary passes.	
	Publicity: Week of March 15th: Send invitations to guidebook writers and newspaper travel editors in eastern Massachusetts for a press weekend in May. Send also to parenting magazines and writers in the Boston area. Also contact other area businesses that would like to cohost the weekend	Mary	$75 for postage and stationery
April	Direct Marketing: Arrange to rent mailing list of tourists from chamber of commerce.	Denise	$70 for list rental Postage: 700 x .29 = $203
	Send letter and brochure for special family weekend in June.		

Month	Media	Execution	Budget
	Advertising: none		
	Publicity: Week of April 1st: Make follow-up calls to editors who received invitation for May weekend.	Mary	$40 (estimated)
May	Direct Marketing: None		
	Advertising: None		
	Publicity: Weekend of 15th: Host press weekend	Mary & Denise	$300 for food, gas, lost room revenue
June	Direct Marketing: For small convention business, go through local corporations, send a letter and brochure.	Denise	$100 for postage and stationery
	Advertising: None		
	Publicity: None		
July	Direct Marketing: None		
	Advertising: Weekly newspaper ad	Mary	4 x $30/per ad = $120
	Publicity: Send press kit to national magazines about your Christmas activities, with photos from last year.	Denise	$80
August	Direct Marketing: None		
	Advertising: Weekly newspaper ad	Mary	4 x $30/per ad = $120
	Publicity: Follow-up calls from July	Denise	$40 phone bill

Month	*Media*	*Execution*	*Budget*
September (busy month)	Direct Marketing: None		
	Advertising: Weekly newspaper ad	Mary	4 x $30/per ad = $120
	Take out ad in winter issue of regional magazine	Mary	$230
	Publicity: None		
	Other: Start planning Christmas week activities with other businesses	Denise	
October	Direct Marketing: Letter to house list for Christmas week— special 5-day packages	Denise	500 x .29 = $145; Stationery: $75
	Other: Scour engage- ment announcements. Send brochure and wedding rates to the couples' parents and offer special discounts for guests.	Denise	10 a week, $50 for month
November (slowest month)	Direct Marketing: None		
	Advertising: Leaf through solicitations for tourism magazines & directories to be published in spring. Take out 1/6 page ad in regional tourism publication.	Mary	$230

Month	Media	Execution	Budget
December	Direct Marketing: None		
	Advertising: Weekly newspaper ad for Christmas activities	Dick	4 x $30/per ad = $120
	Publicity: Call editors to confirm if they'll attend Christmas week activities.	Denise	$40 (estimated)
	Other: Plan Christmas week and help other area businesses with their promotions.		
			Total: $2,942.80

RESOURCES FOR SMALL BUSINESS

Upstart Publishing Company, Inc. These publications on proven management techniques for small businesses are available from Upstart Publishing Company, Inc., 12 Portland St., Dover, NH 03820. For a free current catalog, call (800) 235-8866 outside New Hampshire, or (603) 749-5071 in state.

The Business Planning Guide, 6th edition, 1992, David H. Bangs, Jr. and Upstart Publishing Company, Inc. A manual that helps you write a business plan and financing proposal tailored to your business, your goals and your resources. Includes worksheets and checklists. (Softcover, 208 pp., $19.95)

The Market Planning Guide, 4th edition, 1994, David H. Bangs, Jr. and Upstart Publishing Company, Inc. A manual to help small-business owners put together a goal-oriented, resource-based marketing plan with action steps, benchmarks and time lines. Includes worksheets and checklists to make implementation and review easier. (Softcover, 180 pp., $19.95)

The Cash Flow Control Guide, 1990, David H. Bangs, Jr. and Upstart Publishing Company, Inc. A manual to help small-business owners solve their number one financial problem. Includes worksheets and checklists. (Softcover, 88 pp., $14.95)

The Personnel Planning Guide, 1988, David H. Bangs, Jr. and Upstart Publishing Company, Inc. A 176-page manual outlining practical, proven personnel management techniques, including hiring, managing, evaluating and compensating personnel. Includes worksheets and checklists. (Softcover, 176 pp., $19.95)

The Start Up Guide: A One-Year Plan for Entrepreneurs, 2nd edition, 1994, David H. Bangs, Jr. and Upstart Publishing Company,

Inc. This book utilizes the same step-by-step, no-jargon method as *The Business Planning Guide*, to help even those with no business training through the process of beginning a successful business. (Softcover, 176 pp., $19.95)

Managing By the Numbers: Financial Essentials for the Growing Business, 1992, David H. Bangs, Jr. and Upstart Publishing Company, Inc. Straightforward techniques for getting the maximum return with a minimum of detail in your business's financial management. (Softcover, 160 pp., $19.95.)

Building Wealth, 1992, David H. Bangs, Jr. and the editors of *Common Sense*. A collection of tested techniques designed to help you plan your personal finances and how to plan your business finances to benefit you, your family and employees. (Softcover, 168 pp., $19.95)

Buy the Right Business—At the Right Price, 1990, Brian Knight and the Associates of Country Business, Inc. Many people who would like to be in business for themselves think strictly of starting a business. In some cases, buying a going concern may be preferable—and just as affordable. (Softcover, 152 pp., $18.95)

Borrowing for Your Business, 1991, George M. Dawson. This is a book for borrowers and about lenders. Includes detailed guidelines on how to select a bank and a banker, how to answer the lender's seven most important questions, how your banker looks at a loan and how to get a loan renewed. (Hardcover, 160 pp., $19.95)

Can This Partnership Be Saved?, 1992, Peter Wylie and Mardy Grothe. The authors offer solutions and hope for problems between key people in business. (Softcover, 272 pp., $19.95)

Cases in Small Business Management, 1994, John Edward de Young. A compilation of intriguing and useful case studies in typical small business problems. (Softcover, 258 pp., $24.95)

The Complete Guide to Selling Your Business, 1992, Paul Sperry and Beatrice Mitchell. A step-by-step guide through the entire process from how to determine when the time is right to sell to negotiating the final terms. (Hardcover, 160 pp., $21.95)

The Complete Selling System, 1991, Pete Frye. This book can help any manager or salesperson, even those with no experience, find the solutions to some of the most common dilemmas in managing sales. (Hardcover, 192 pp., $21.95)

Creating Customers, 1992, David H. Bangs, Jr. and the editors of *Common Sense*. A book for business owners and managers who want a step-by-step approach to selling and promoting. Techniques include inexpensive market research, pricing your goods and services and writing a usable marketing plan. (Softcover, 176 pp., $19.95)

The Entrepreneur's Guide to Going Public, 1994, James B. Arkebauer with Ron Schultz. A comprehensive and useful book on a subject that is the ultimate dream of most entrepreneurs—making an initial public offering IPO). (Softcover, 368 pp., $19.95)

Export Profits, 1992, Jack S. Wolf. This book shows how to find the right foreign markets for your product, cut through the red tape, minimize currency risks and how to find the experts who can help. (Softcover, 304 pp., $19.95)

Financial Troubleshooting, 1992, David H. Bangs, Jr. and the editors of *Common Sense*. This book helps the owner/ manger use basic diagnostic methods to monitor the health of the business and solve problems before damage occurs. (Softcover, 192 pp., $19.95)

Financial Essentials for Small Business Success, 1994, Joseph Tabet and Jeffrey Slater. Designed to show readers where to get the information they need and how planning and recordkeeping will enhance the health of any small business. (Softcover, 272 pp., $19.95)

From Kitchen to Market, 1992, Stephen Hall. A practical approach to turning culinary skills into a profitable business. (Softcover, 208 pp., $24.95)

The Home-Based Entrepreneur, 1993, Linda Pinson and Jerry Jinnett. A step-by-step guide to all the issues surrounding starting a home-based business. Issues such as zoning, labor laws and licensing are discussed and forms are provided to get you on your way. (Softcover, 192 pp. $19.95)

Keeping the Books, 1993, Linda Pinson and Jerry Jinnett. Basic business recordkeeping both explained and illustrated. Designed to give you a clear understanding of small business accounting by taking you step-by-step through general records, development of financial statements, tax reporting, scheduling and financial statement analysis. (Softcover, 208 pp., $19.95)

The Language of Small Business, 1994, Carl O. Trautmann. A clear, concise dictionary of small business terms for students and small business owners. (Softcover, 416 pp., $19.95)

Marketing Your Invention, 1992, Thomas Mosley. This book dispels the myths and clearly communicates what inventors need to know to successfully bring their inventions to market. (Softcover, 232 pp., $19.95)

100 Best Retirement Businesses, 1994, Lisa Angowski Rogak with David H. Bangs, Jr. A one-of-a-kind book bringing retirees the inside information on the most interesting and most lucrative businesses for them. (Softcover, 416 pp., $15.95)

The Small Business Computer Book, 1993, Robert Moskowitz. This book does not recommend particular systems, but rather provides readers with a way to think about these choices and make the right decisions for their businesses. (Softcover, 190 pp., $19.95)

Start Your Own Business for $1,000 or Less, 1994, Will Davis. Shows readers how to get started in the "mini-business" of their dreams with less than $1,000. (Softcover, 280 pp., $17.95)

Steps to Small Business Start-Up, 1993, Linda Pinson and Jerry Jinnett. A step-by-step guide for starting and succeeding with a small or home-based business. Takes you through the mechanics of business start-up and gives an overview of information on such topics as copyrights, trademarks, legal structures, recordkeeping and marketing. (Softcover, 256 pp., $19.95)

Target Marketing for the Small Business, 1993, Linda Pinson and Jerry Jinnett. A comprehensive guide to marketing your business. This book not only shows you how to reach your customers, it also gives you a wealth of information on how to research that market through the use of library resources, questionnaires, demographics, etc. (Softcover, 176 pp., $19.95)

On Your Own: A Woman's Guide to Starting Your Own Business, 2nd edition, 1993, Laurie Zuckerman. *On Your Own* is for women who want hands-on, practical information about starting and running their own business. It deals honestly with issues like finding time for your business when you're also the primary care provider, societal biases against women and credit discrimination. (Softcover, 320 pp., $19.95)

Problem Employees, 1991, Dr. Peter Wylie and Dr. Mardy Grothe. Provides managers and supervisors with a simple, practical and straightforward approach to help all employees, especially problem employees, significantly improve their work performance. (Softcover, 272 pp., $22.95)

Problems and Solutions in Small Business Management, 1994, The Editors of *Forum,* the journal of the Association of Small Business Development Centers. A collection of case studies selected from the pages of *Forum* magazine. (Softcover, 200 pp., $21.95)

The Restaurant Planning Guide, 1992, Peter Rainsford and David H. Bangs, Jr. This book takes the practical techniques of *The Business Planning Guide* and combines it with the expertise of Peter Rainsford, a professor at the Cornell School of Hotel Administration and restaurateur. Topics include: establishing menu prices, staffing and scheduling, controlling costs and niche marketing. (Softcover, 176 pp., $19.95)

Successful Retailing, 2nd edition, 1993, Paula Wardell. Provides hands-on help for those who want to start or expand their retail business. Sections include: strategic planning, marketing and market research and inventory control. (Softcover, 176 pp., $19.95)

The Upstart Guide to Owning and Managing an Antiques Business, 1994, Lisa Angowski Rogak. Provides the information a prospective antiques dealer needs to run a business profitably. (Softcover, 250 pp., $15.95)

The Upstart Guide to Owning and Managing a Bar or Tavern, 1994, Roy Alonzo. Provides essential information on planning, making the initial investment, financial management and marketing a bar or tavern. (Softcover, 250 pp., $15.95)

The Upstart Guide to Owning and Managing a Desktop Publishing Service, 1994, Dan Ramsey. How to take advantage of desktop computer equipment and turn it into a thriving business. (Softcover, 250 pp., $15.95)

The Upstart Guide to Owning and Managing a Resume Service, 1994, Dan Ramsey. Shows how any reader can turn personnel, writing and computer skills into a lucrative resume-writing business. (Softcover, 250 pp., $15.95)

The Woman Entrepreneur, 1992, Linda Pinson and Jerry Jinnett. Thirty-three successful women business owners share their practical ideas for success and their sources for inspiration. (Softcover, 244 pp., $14.00)

Other Available Titles

The Complete Guide to Business Agreements, 1993, Ted Nicholas, Enterprise • Dearborn. Contains 127 of the most commonly needed business agreements. (Loose-leaf binder, $69.95)

The Complete Small Business Legal Guide, 1993, Robert Friedman, Enterprise • Dearborn. Provides the hands-on help you need to start a business, maintain all necessary records, properly hire and fire employees and deal with the many changes a business goes through. (Softcover, $69.95)

Forecasting Sales and Planning Profits: A No-Nonsense Guide for Growing a Business, 1986, Kenneth E. Marino, Probus Publishing Co. Concise and easily applied forecasting system based on an analysis of market potential and sale requirements, which helps establish the basis for financial statements in your business plan. Book is currently out of print, check second-hand bookstores for the title.

Guerrilla Marketing: Secrets for Making Big Profits from Your Small Business, 1984, J. Conrad Levinson, Houghton-Mifflin. A classic tool kit for small businesses. (Hardcover, 226 pp., $14.95)

How to Form Your Own Corporation Without a Lawyer for Under $75.00, 1992, Ted Nicholas, Enterprise • Dearborn. A good book for helping you to discover all the unique advantages of incorporating while at the same time learning how quick, easy and inexpensive the process can be. (Softcover, $19.95)

Marketing Sourcebook for Small Business, 1989, Jeffrey P. Davidson, John Wylie Publishing. A good introductory book for small business owners with excellent definitions of important marketing terms and concepts. (Hardcover, 325 pp., $24.95)

The Small Business Survival Kit: 101 Troubleshooting Tips for Success, 1993, John Ventura, Enterprise • Dearborn. Offers compassionate insight into the emotional side of financial difficulties as well as a nuts and bolts consideration of options for the small businessperson experiencing tough times. (Softcover, $19.95)

INDEX